Level II Schweser's Secret Sauce®

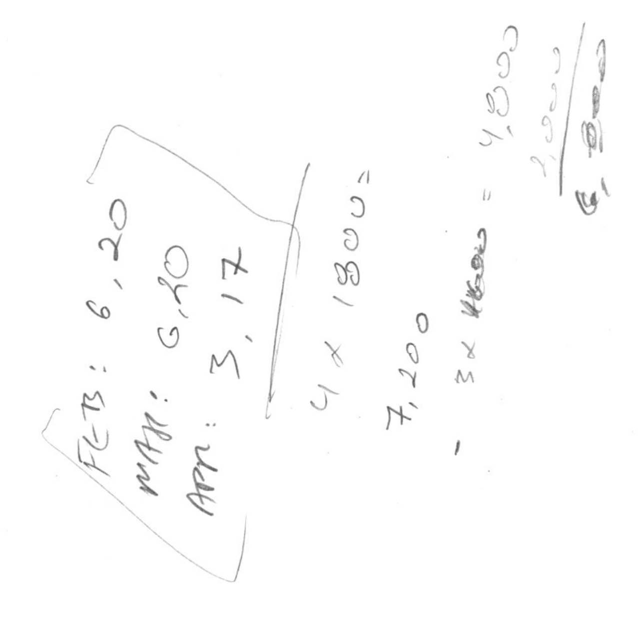

SCHWESER'S SECRET SAUCE®: 2013 CFA LEVEL II

Published in 2013 by Kaplan Schweser.

Printed in the United States of America.

ISBN: 978-1-4277-4240-7 / 1-4277-4240-5

PPN: 3200-2877

Foreword

Secret Sauce® is a valuable addition to the study tools of any CFA exam candidate. It offers very concise and very readable explanations of the major parts of the Level II CFA curriculum.

This book does not cover every Learning Outcome Statement (LOS) and, as you are aware, any LOS is "fair game" for the exam. We focus here on those LOS that are core concepts in finance and accounting, have application to other LOS, are complex and difficult for candidates, or require memorization of characteristics or relationships.

Secret Sauce is easier to carry with you and will allow you to study these key concepts, definitions, and techniques over and over, an important part of mastering the material. When you get to topics where the coverage here appears too brief or raises questions in your mind, this is your clue to go back to your study notes to fill in the gaps in your understanding. There is no shortcut to learning the very broad array of subject matter covered by the Level II curriculum, but this volume should be a very valuable tool for learning and reviewing the material as you progress in your studies over the months leading up to exam day.

Pass rates remain around 40%, and returning Level II candidates make comments such as, "I was surprised at how difficult the exam was." You should not despair because of this, but you should also not underestimate this challenge. Our study materials, practice exams, test bank, videos, seminars, and Secret Sauce are all designed to help you study as efficiently as possible, grasp and retain the material, and apply it with confidence on exam day.

Best regards,

Bijesh Tolia

Dr. Bijesh Tolia, CFA, CA
Vice President of CFA Education
and Level II Manager
Kaplan Schweser

Kent Westlund

Kent Westlund, CFA
Content Specialist

Ethical and Professional Standards

Study Sessions 1 & 2

Topic Weight on Exam	10%
SchweserNotes™ Reference	Book 1, Pages 13–137

For many candidates, ethics is the most difficult material to master. Even though you are an ethical person, you will not be prepared to perform well on this portion of the Level II exam without a comprehensive knowledge of the Standards of Professional Conduct.

Ten percent of the points come from the ethics material, so you should view this topic as an area where you can set yourself apart from the person sitting next to you in the exam room. CFA Institute has indicated that performance on the ethics material serves as a "tie-breaker" for exam scores very close to the minimum passing score. This is referred to as the "ethics adjustment."

What's the point? *The ethics material is worth taking seriously*. With 10% of the points and the possibility of pushing a marginal exam into the pass column (not to mention the fact that as a candidate you are obligated to abide by CFA Institute Standards), it is foolhardy not to devote the needed time to ethics.

A Study Plan for Ethics

The big question is, "What do I need to know?" The answer is that you really need to know all the ethics material. You simply must spend time learning the Standards and developing some intuition about how CFA Institute expects you to respond on the exam. Here are several quick guidelines to help in your preparation:

- *Focus on the Standards*. The Standards of Professional Conduct are the key to the ethics material. The Code of Ethics is a poetic statement of objectives, but the heart of the testing comes from the Standards.

- *Broad interpretation.* A broad definition of most standards is needed for testing purposes *even if it seems too broad to apply in your "real world" situation.* For instance, a key component of the professional standards is the concept of disclosure (e.g., disclosure of conflicts of interest, compensation plans, and soft dollar arrangements). On the exam, you need to interpret what needs to be disclosed very broadly. A good guideline is that if there is any question in your mind about whether a particular bit of information needs to be disclosed, then it most certainly needs disclosing. *Err on the side of massive disclosure!*
- *Always side with the employer.* Many view the Code and Standards to be an employer-oriented document. That is, for many readers the employer's interests seem to be more amply protected. If there is a potential conflict between the employee and employer, always side with the employer.
- *Defend the charter.* CFA Institute views itself as the guardian of the industry's reputation and, specifically, the guardian of the CFA® designation. On the exam, be very suspicious of activity that makes industry professionals and CFA charterholders look bad.
- *Assume all investors are inexperienced.* Many different scenarios can show up on the exam (e.g., a money manager contemplating a trade for a large trust fund). However, when you study this material, view the Standards from the perspective of a money manager with fiduciary responsibility for a small account belonging to inexperienced investors. Assuming that the investors are inexperienced makes some issues more clear.

Now, how should you approach this material? There are two keys here.

- *First, you need to read the material very carefully.* We suggest that you underline key words and concepts and commit them to memory. It's probably a good idea to start your study effort with a careful read of ethics and then go over the material again in May.
- *Second, you should answer every practice ethics question you can get your hands on to develop some intuition.* The truth is that on the exam, you are going to encounter a number of ethics questions that you don't immediately know the answer to. Answering a lot of practice questions will help you develop some intuition about how CFA Institute expects you to interpret the ethical situations on the exam. Also, study every example in the *Standards of Practice Handbook* and be prepared for questions on the exam that test similar concepts.

Code of Ethics

Cross-Reference to CFA Institute Assigned Topic Review #1

Members of the CFA Institute and candidates for the CFA designation must:

- Act with integrity, competence, diligence, respect, and in an ethical manner with the public, clients, prospective clients, employers, employees, colleagues in the investment profession, and other participants in the global capital markets.

- Place the integrity of the investment profession and the interests of clients above their own personal interests.
- Use reasonable care and exercise independent professional judgment when conducting investment analysis, making investment recommendations, taking investment actions, and engaging in other professional activities.
- Practice and encourage others to practice in a professional and ethical manner that will reflect credit on themselves and the profession.
- Promote the integrity of, and uphold the rules governing, capital markets.
- Maintain and improve their professional competence and strive to maintain and improve the competence of other investment professionals.

Standards of Professional Conduct

Cross-Reference to CFA Institute Assigned Topic Review #2

The following is a summary of the Standards of Professional Conduct. Focus on the purpose of the standard, applications of the standard, and proper procedures of compliance for each standard.

Standard I: Professionalism

I(A) **Knowledge of the Law.** Understand and comply with laws, rules, regulations, and Code and Standards of any authority governing your activities. In the event of a conflict, follow the more strict law, rule, or regulation. Do not knowingly participate or assist in violations, and dissociate from any known violation.

Professor's Note: The requirement to disassociate from any violations committed by others is explicit in the Standard. This might mean resigning from the firm in extreme cases. The guidance statement also makes clear that you aren't required to report potential violations of the Code and Standards committed by other members or candidates to CFA Institute, although it is encouraged. Compliance with any applicable fiduciary duties to clients would now be covered under this standard.

I(B) **Independence and Objectivity.** Use reasonable care to exercise independence and objectivity in professional activities. Don't offer, solicit, or accept any gift, benefit, compensation, or consideration that would compromise either your own or someone else's independence and objectivity.

Professor's Note: The prohibition against accepting gifts, benefits, compensation, or other consideration that might compromise your independence and objectivity includes all situations beyond just those involving clients and prospects, including investment banking relationships, public companies the analyst is following, pressure on sell-side analysts by buy-side clients, and issuer-paid research.

I(C) **Misrepresentation.** Do not knowingly misrepresent facts regarding investment analysis, recommendations, actions, or other professional activities.

Professor's Note: Plagiarism is addressed under the broader category of misrepresentation.

I(D) **Misconduct.** Do not engage in any professional conduct that involves dishonesty, fraud, or deceit. Do not do anything that reflects poorly on your integrity, good reputation, trustworthiness, or professional competence.

Professor's Note: The scope of this standard addresses only professional misconduct and not personal misconduct. There is no attempt to overreach or regulate one's personal behavior.

Standard II: Integrity of Capital Markets

II(A) **Material Nonpublic Information.** If you are in possession of nonpublic information that could affect an investment's value, do not act or induce someone else to act on the information.

Professor's Note: This Standard addressing insider trading states that members and candidates must not act or cause others to act on material nonpublic information until that same information is made public. This is a strict standard—it does not matter whether the information is obtained in breach of a duty, is misappropriated, or relates to a tender offer. The "mosaic theory" still applies, and an analyst can take action based on her analysis of public and nonmaterial nonpublic information.

II(B) **Market Manipulation.** Do not engage in any practices intended to mislead market participants through distorted prices or artificially inflated trading volume.

Standard III: Duties to Clients

III(A) **Loyalty, Prudence, and Care.** Always act for the benefit of clients and place clients' interests before your employer's or your own interests. You must be loyal to clients, use reasonable care, and exercise prudent judgment.

Professor's Note: Applicability of any fiduciary duties to clients and prospects is now covered under Standard I(A) Knowledge of the Law.

III(B) **Fair Dealing.** You must deal fairly and objectively with all clients and prospects when providing investment analysis, making investment recommendations, taking investment action, or in other professional activities.

Professor's Note: This Standard includes providing investment analysis and engaging in other professional activities as well as disseminating investment recommendations and taking investment action.

III(C) **Suitability**

1. When in an advisory relationship with a client or prospect, you must:
    - Make reasonable inquiry into a client's investment experience, risk and return objectives, and constraints prior to making any recommendations or taking investment action. Reassess information and update regularly.
    - Be sure investments are suitable to a client's financial situation and consistent with client objectives before making recommendations or taking investment action.
    - Make sure investments are suitable in the context of a client's total portfolio.
2. When managing a portfolio, your investment recommendations and actions must be consistent with the stated portfolio objectives and constraints.

Professor's Note: The client's written objectives and constraints are required to be reviewed and updated "regularly." The second item applies the suitability standard to managed portfolios and requires you to stick to the mandated investment style as outlined in the portfolio objectives and constraints.

III(D) **Performance Presentation.** Presentations of investment performance information must be fair, accurate, and complete.

III(E) **Preservation of Confidentiality.** All information about current and former clients and prospects must be kept confidential unless it pertains to illegal activities, disclosure is required by law, or the client or prospect gives permission for the information to be disclosed.

Professor's Note: This Standard covers all client information, not just information concerning matters within the scope of the relationship. Also note that the language specifically includes not only prospects but former clients. Confidentiality regarding employer information is covered in Standard IV.

Standard IV: Duties to Employers

IV(A) **Loyalty**. You must place your employer's interest before your own and must not deprive your employer of your skills and abilities, divulge confidential information, or otherwise harm your employer.

Professor's Note: The phrase "in matters related to employment" means that you are not required to subordinate important personal and family obligations to your job. The Standard also addresses the issue of "whistle-blowing" by stating that there are circumstances in which the employer's interests are subordinated to actions necessary to protect the integrity of the capital markets or client interests.

IV(B) **Additional Compensation Arrangements**. No gifts, benefits, compensation, or consideration that may create a conflict of interest with the employer's interest are to be accepted, unless written consent is received from all parties.

Professor's Note: "Compensation" includes "gifts, benefits, compensation, or consideration."

IV(C) **Responsibilities of Supervisors**. You must make reasonable efforts to detect and prevent violations of laws, rules, regulations, and the Code and Standards by any person under your supervision or authority.

Professor's Note: The focus is on establishing and implementing reasonable compliance procedures in order to meet this Standard. Notice also that informing your employer of your responsibility to abide by the Code and Standards is only a recommendation.

Standard V: Investment Analysis, Recommendations, and Actions

V(A) **Diligence and Reasonable Basis**

1. When analyzing investments, making recommendations, and taking investment actions, use diligence, independence, and thoroughness.
2. Investment analysis, recommendations, and actions should have a reasonable and adequate basis, supported by research and investigation.

Professor's Note: This Standard explicitly requires that you exercise diligence and have a reasonable basis for investment analysis, as well as for making recommendations or taking investment action.

V(B) Communication With Clients and Prospective Clients

1. Disclose to clients and prospects the basic format and general principles of investment processes used to analyze and select securities and construct portfolios. Promptly disclose any process changes.
2. Use reasonable judgment in identifying relevant factors important to investment analyses, recommendations, or actions, and include those factors when communicating with clients and prospects.
3. Investment analyses and recommendations should clearly differentiate facts from opinions.

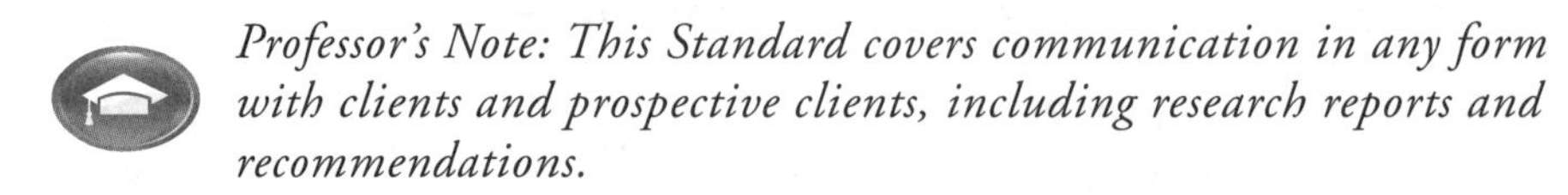
Professor's Note: This Standard covers communication in any form with clients and prospective clients, including research reports and recommendations.

V(C) Record Retention. Maintain all records supporting analysis, recommendations, actions, and all other investment-related communications with clients and prospects.

Professor's Note: The issue of record retention is a separate Standard, emphasizing its importance. It includes records relating to investment analysis as well as investment recommendations and actions. The guidance statement says you should maintain records for seven years in the absence of other regulatory guidance.

Standard VI: Conflicts of Interest

VI(A) Disclosure of Conflicts. You must make full and fair disclosure of all matters that may impair your independence or objectivity or interfere with your duties to employer, clients, and prospects. Disclosures must be prominent, in plain language, and effectively communicate the information.

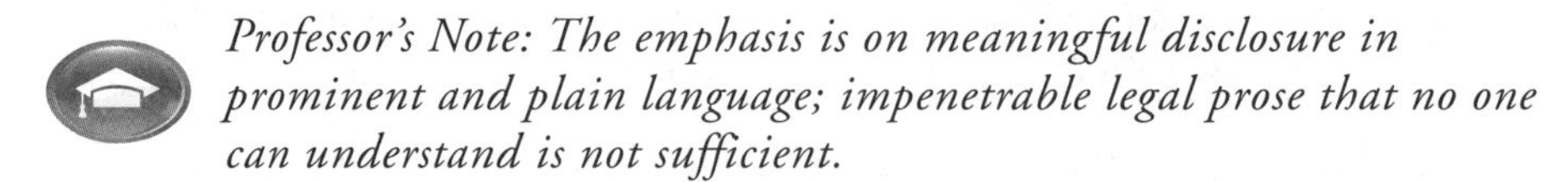
Professor's Note: The emphasis is on meaningful disclosure in prominent and plain language; impenetrable legal prose that no one can understand is not sufficient.

VI(B) Priority of Transactions. Investment transactions for clients and employers must have priority over those in which you are a beneficial owner.

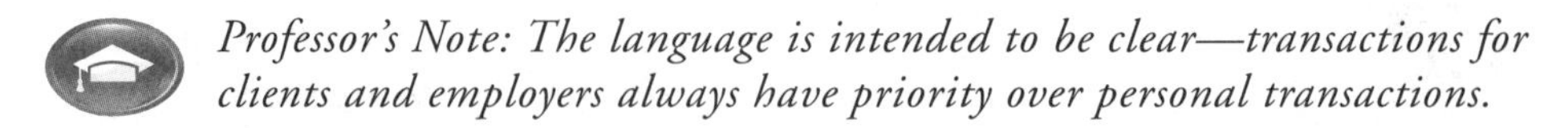
Professor's Note: The language is intended to be clear—transactions for clients and employers always have priority over personal transactions.

VI(C) Referral Fees. You must disclose to your employers, clients, and prospects any compensation, consideration, or benefit received by, or paid to, others for recommendations of products and services.

Standard VII: Responsibilities as a CFA Institute Member or CFA Candidate

VII(A) **Conduct as Members and Candidates in the CFA Program.** You must not engage in conduct that compromises the reputation or integrity of CFA Institute, the CFA designation, or the integrity, validity, or security of the CFA exams.

Professor's Note: The Standard is intended to cover conduct such as cheating on the CFA exam or otherwise violating rules of CFA Institute or the CFA program. It is not intended to prevent anyone from expressing any opinions or beliefs concerning CFA Institute or the CFA program. Violations also include discussing the questions (or even broad subject areas) that were tested or not tested on the exam.

VII(B) **Reference to CFA Institute, the CFA Designation, and the CFA Program.** You must not misrepresent or exaggerate the meaning or implications of membership in CFA Institute, holding the CFA designation, or candidacy in the program.

Professor's Note: This Standard prohibits you from engaging in any conduct that may "misrepresent or exaggerate the meaning or implications of membership in CFA Institute, holding the CFA designation, or candidacy in the CFA program." You cannot reference any "partial" designation, since this also misrepresents or exaggerates credentials.

Other Level II Ethics Topic Reviews

The Code and Standards are the heart of the Level II ethics curriculum, so we recommend spending about 60% of your ethics study time on them. However, some additional ethics topic reviews at Level II may be tested, including the CFA Institute Soft Dollar Standards, the CFA Institute Research Objectivity Standards, and the New Prudent Investor Rule. Spend the other 40% of your time on these topics and focus on the key points discussed in the following sections. Remember that the Research Objectivity Standards are applicable only to firms (as opposed to individuals) who claim compliance.

CFA Institute Soft Dollar Standards

Cross-Reference to CFA Institute Assigned Topic Review #3

"Soft dollars" (or "client brokerage") refers to investment research, products and services, and cash credits given to the investment manager by brokers in return for client business. The soft dollar credit is the client's asset because he pays the commission. Fiduciaries owe their clients two basic duties: to act in the client's best interest and to disclose conflicts of interest. The cardinal rule is that soft dollars are an asset of the client, and soft dollars may not be used for any purpose that does not benefit that client.

Know the two key principles of the Soft Dollar Standards and apply them to any question in which you are unsure of the specific details of the Standards.

- Principle #1: Brokerage is the property of the client.
- Principle #2: Investment managers have a duty to obtain best execution, minimize transactions costs, and use client brokerage to benefit clients.

You should be familiar with some of the key requirements of the Soft Dollar Standards, as outlined in Figure 1.

Figure 1: Key Requirements of the CFA Institute Soft Dollar Standards

Category	*Key Requirements*
General	• Place client interests above all else. • Don't allocate client brokerage based on client referrals from brokers.
Relationships With Clients	• Disclose potential participation in soft dollar arrangements.
Selection of Brokers	• Consider brokers' trade execution capabilities when selecting brokers.
Evaluation of Research	• Use client brokerage only for products and services that meet the definition of "research": products and services that assist the investment manager in the investment decision-making process. • Document basis for determining why it meets the definition. • Research must benefit the client. • Allocate research cost based on expected usage for mixed-use research.
Client-Directed Brokerage	• Don't use brokerage from one client to pay for research purchased for another client who is operating under a client-directed brokerage agreement.
Disclosure	• Disclose policies in plan language. • Send clients annual statement that soft dollar practices conform to Soft Dollar Standards. • Disclose to clients that more information on policies is available upon request.
Record Keeping	• Meet all regulatory and legal requirements. • Document any specific arrangement with clients, including client-directed brokerage agreements. • Document the basis for mixed-use allocations. • Document how products and services assist the manager in the investment decision-making process. • Document compliance with the Soft Dollar Standards.

CFA Institute Research Objectivity Standards

Cross-Reference to CFA Institute Assigned Topic Review #4

The Research Objectivity Standards are voluntary standards intended to complement and facilitate compliance with the Standards of Practice. They are intended to be a universal guide for all investment firms by providing ethical standards and practices regarding full and fair disclosure of any conflicts or potential conflicts relating to the firm's research and investment recommendations. However, firms are not required to comply with the Research Objectivity Standards.

Professor's Note: If you have an understanding of the basic requirements, you should be able to handle most of the questions on the topic that might appear on the Level II exam. We also suggest that you review the Recommended Procedures for Compliance.

Figure 2: Key Requirements of the CFA Institute Research Objectivity Standards

Category	*Key Requirements*
Research Objectivity Policy	• Have a formal, written policy and distribute it to clients, prospective clients, and employees. • Senior office must attest annually that firm complies with policy.
Public Appearances	• Disclose conflicts of interest when discussing research and recommendations in public forums.
Reasonable and Adequate Basis	• All reports and recommendations must have a reasonable and adequate basis.
Investment Banking	• Separate research analysts from investment banking. • Don't let analysts report to, or be supervised by, investment banking personnel. • Don't let investment banking review, revise, or approve research reports and recommendations.
Research Analyst Compensation	• Link analyst compensation to quality of analysis, not amount of investment banking business done with client.
Relationships With Subject Companies	• Don't let subject companies see issue rating or recommendation prior to release, or promise a specific rating or recommendation.
Personal Investments and Trading	• Don't engage in front running of client trades. • Don't let employees and immediate family members trade ahead of clients, trade contrary to firm recommendations, or participate in IPOs of companies covered by the firm.
Timeliness of Research Reports and Recommendations	• Issue research reports on a timely basis.
Compliance and Enforcement	• Enforce policies and compliance procedures, assess disciplinary sanctions, monitor effectiveness of procedures, and maintain records.
Disclosure	• Disclose conflicts of interest.
Rating System	• Have a rating system that investors find useful and provide them with information they can use to determine suitability.

The New Prudent Investor Rule

Cross-Reference to CFA Institute Assigned Topic Review #10

Differences Between the Old Prudent Man Rule and the New Prudent Investor Rule

The new Prudent Investor Rule makes five key changes to the traditional rules governing investment trust management.

- *Use of total return.* The new Rule measures reasonable portfolio return as total return (income plus capital growth) and emphasizes that the trustee's duty is to not only preserve the purchasing power of the trust but, in certain cases, to realize principal growth in excess of inflation.
- *Risk management.* Under the new Rule, the trustee has the obligation to assess the risk and return objectives of the trust beneficiaries and manage the trust in a prudent manner consistent with those objectives, rather than to avoid all risk.
- *Evaluation in a portfolio context.* While the new Rule calls for the avoidance of undue speculation and risk, it also encourages trustees to view risk in a portfolio context.
- *Security restrictions.* No securities are "off-limits" because of their riskiness when held in isolation. For example, under the old Rule, options were not allowed, but under the new Rule, they are, as long as the manager takes the portfolio perspective to analyzing risk.
- *Delegation of duty.* The old Rule did not permit trustees to delegate investment authority. In fact, investing in mutual funds or even index funds was deemed improper. The new Rule goes so far as to say that it may be the duty of a trustee (this is stronger language than just authority) to delegate, just as a prudent investor would.

Professor's Note: These principles are consistent with the guidelines outlined in the topic review of the portfolio management process in Study Session 18, where the LOS ask you to explain the importance of the portfolio perspective and define investment objectives and constraints.

Key Factors That Trustees Should Consider

The new Prudent Investor Rule includes eight key factors that the trustee should consider when investing and managing trust assets:

1. Economic conditions.
2. Effects of inflation and deflation.
3. Impact of investment decisions on the beneficiary's tax liability.
4. How each individual investment contributes to the risk and return of the overall portfolio.
5. Expected total return from capital appreciation and income.
6. Other resources of the beneficiary.
7. The beneficiary's liquidity, income, and capital preservation requirements.
8. Whether any assets have a special relationship to the requirements of the beneficiary or the trust.

QUANTITATIVE METHODS

Study Session 3

Topic Weight on Exam	5–10%
SchweserNotes™ Reference	Book 1, Pages 138–261

Quantitative analysis is one of the primary tools used in the investment community, so you can expect CFA Institute to test this section thoroughly. Both linear regression (with only one independent variable) and multiple regression (with more than one independent variable) are covered in the Level II Quant readings. The Level II curriculum also includes a topic review on time series analysis.

A key topic in the Level II Quant material is multiple regression. If you have a solid understanding of simple linear regression, you can handle multiple regression and anything you might see on the Level II exam. All the important concepts in simple linear regression are repeated in the context of multiple regression (e.g., testing regression parameters and calculating predicted values of the dependent variable), and you're most likely to see these tested as part of a multiple regression question.

For the time series material, the concepts of nonstationarity, unit roots (i.e., random walks), and serial correlation, will be important, as well as being able to calculate the mean-reverting level of an autoregressive (AR) time-series model. Understand the implications of seasonality and how to detect and correct it, as well as the root mean squared error (RMSE) as a model evaluation criterion.

CORRELATION AND REGRESSION

Cross-Reference to CFA Institute Assigned Topic Review #11

Because everything you learn for simple linear regression can be applied to multiple linear regression, you should focus on the material presented in the next section. The only topics unique to simple linear regression are (1) the correlation coefficient, (2) regression assumptions, and (3) forming a prediction interval for the dependent (Y) variable.

Correlation Coefficient

The *correlation coefficient, r,* for a sample and ρ for a population, is a measure of the strength of the linear relationship (correlation) between two variables. A correlation coefficient with a value of +1 indicates that two variables move exactly together (perfect positive correlation), a value of –1 indicates that the variables move exactly opposite (perfect negative correlation), and a value of 0 indicates no linear relationship.

The test statistic for the significance of a correlation coefficient (null is $\rho = 0$) has a *t*-distribution with n – 2 degrees of freedom and is calculated as:

$$t = \frac{r\sqrt{n-2}}{\sqrt{1-r^2}}$$

Regression Assumptions

- A *linear relationship* exists between the dependent and independent variables.
- The *independent variable is uncorrelated with the residual term.*
- The expected value of the *residual term is zero.*
- There is a *constant variance* of the residual term.
- The *residual term is independently distributed*; that is, the residual term for one observation is not correlated with that of another observation (a violation of this assumption is called autocorrelation).
- The *residual term is normally distributed.*

Note that five of the six assumptions are related to the residual term. The residual terms are independently (of each other and the independent variable), identically, and normally distributed with a zero mean.

Confidence Interval for a Predicted Y-Value

In simple linear regression, you have to know how to *calculate a confidence interval for the predicted Y value:*

predicted Y value ± (critical t-value)(standard error of forecast)

Calculating a confidence interval for the predicted *y* value is *not* part of the multiple regression LOS, however, because the multiple regression version is too complicated and not part of the Level II curriculum.

Multiple Regression and Issues in Regression Analysis

Cross-Reference to CFA Institute Assigned Topic Review #12

Multiple regression is the most important part of the quant material. You can fully expect that multiple regression will be on the exam, probably in several places.

The flow chart in Figure 1 will help you evaluate a multiple regression model and grasp the "big picture" in preparation for the exam.

Figure 1: Assessment of a Multiple Regression Model

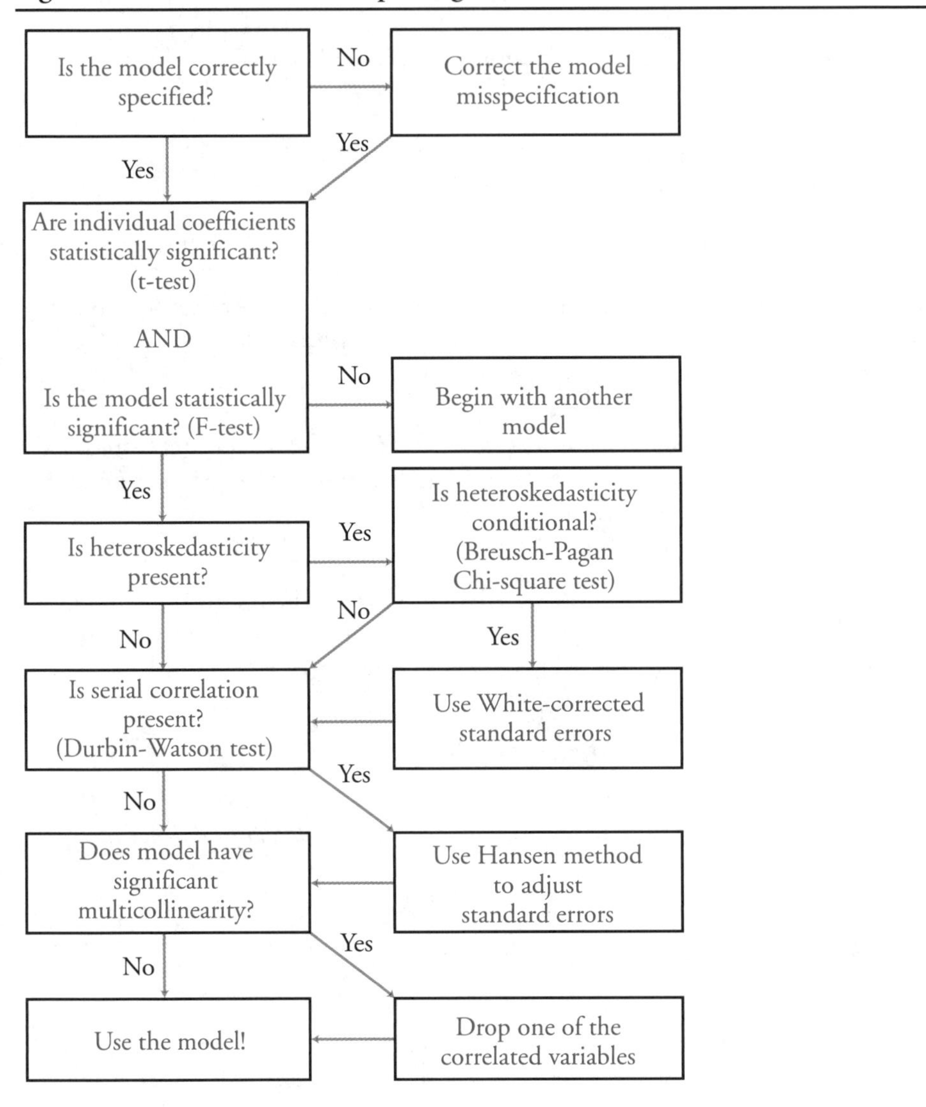

You should know that a *t*-test assesses the statistical significance of the individual regression parameters, and an *F*-test assesses the effectiveness of the model as a whole in explaining the dependent variable. You should understand the effect that heteroskedasticity, serial correlation, and multicollinearity have on regression results. *Focus on interpretation of the regression equation and the test statistics.*

A regression of a dependent variable (e.g., sales) on three independent variables would yield an equation like the following:

$$Y_i = b_0 + (b_1 \times X_{1i}) + (b_2 \times X_{2i}) + (b_3 \times X_{3i}) + \varepsilon_i$$

You should be able to interpret a multiple regression equation, test the slope coefficients for statistical significance, and use an estimated equation to forecast (predict) the value of the dependent variable. Remember, when you are forecasting a value for the dependent variable, you use estimated values for all the independent variables, even those independent variables whose slope coefficient is not statistically different from zero.

Multiple Regression: Testing

Tests for significance in multiple regression involve testing whether:

- Each independent variable *individually* contributes to explaining the variation in the dependent variable using the *t*-statistic.
- Some or all of the independent variables contribute to explaining the variation in the dependent variable using the *F*-statistic.

Tests for individual coefficients. We conduct hypothesis testing on the estimated slope coefficients to determine if the independent variables make a significant contribution to explaining the variation in the dependent variable. With multiple regression, *the critical* t-*stat is distributed with n – k – 1 degrees of freedom*, where *n* is the number of observations and *k* is the number of independent variables.

$$t = \frac{\text{estimated regression parameter}}{\text{standard error of regression parameter}} \text{ with } n - k - 1 \text{ df}$$

ANOVA is a statistical procedure that attributes the variation in the dependent variable to one of two sources: the regression model or the residuals (i.e., the error term). The structure of an ANOVA table is shown in Figure 2.

Figure 2: Analysis of Variance (ANOVA) Table

Source	*df* *(Degrees of Freedom)*	*SS* *(Sum of Squares)*	*MS* *(Mean Square = SS/df)*
Regression	k	RSS	$MSR = \frac{RSS}{k}$
Error	n – k – 1	SSE	$MSE = \frac{SSE}{n-k-1}$
Total	n – 1	SST	

Note that RSS + SSE = SST. The information in an ANOVA table can be used to calculate R^2, the *F*-statistics, and the standard error of estimate (SEE).

The *coefficient of determination* (R^2) is the percentage of the variation in the dependent variable explained by the independent variables.

$$R^2 = \frac{\text{regression sum of squares (RSS)}}{\text{total sum of squares (SST)}}$$

$$= \frac{\text{SST} - \text{sum of squared errors (SSE)}}{\text{SST}}$$

In multiple regression, you also need to understand *adjusted* R^2. The adjusted R^2 provides a measure of the goodness of fit that adjusts for the number of independent variables included in the model.

The *standard error of estimate* (SEE) measures the uncertainty of the values of the dependent variable around the regression line. It is approximately equal to the standard deviation of the residuals. If the relationship between the dependent and independent variables is very strong, the SEE will be low.

$$\text{standard error of estimate (SEE)} = \sqrt{\text{mean squared error (MSE)}}$$

Tests of all coefficients collectively. For this test, the null hypothesis is that all the slope coefficients simultaneously equal zero. The required test is a one-tailed *F*-test and the calculated statistic is:

$$F = \frac{\text{regression mean square (MSR)}}{\text{mean squared error (MSE)}} \text{ with k and n} - \text{k} - 1 \text{ df}$$

The *F*-statistic has two distinct degrees of freedom, one associated with the numerator (*k*, the number of independent variables) and one associated with the denominator (n – k – 1). The critical value is taken from an *F*-table. The decision rule for the *F*-test is reject H_0 if $F > F_{critical}$. *Remember that this is always a one-tailed test.*

Rejection of the null hypothesis at a stated level of significance indicates that at least one of the coefficients is significantly different than zero, which is interpreted to mean that at least one of the independent variables in the regression model makes a significant contribution to the explanation of the dependent variable.

Confidence Intervals

The confidence interval for a regression coefficient in a multiple regression is calculated and interpreted exactly the same as with a simple linear regression:

regression coefficient ± (critical t-value)(standard error of regression coefficient)

If zero is contained in the confidence interval constructed for a coefficient at a desired significance level, we conclude that the slope is not statistically different from zero.

Potential Problems in Regression Analysis

You should be familiar with the three violations of the assumptions of multiple regression and their effects.

Figure 3: Problems in Regression Analysis

	Conditional Heteroskedasticity	*Serial Correlation*	*Multicollinearity*
What is it?	Residual variance related to level of independent variables	Residuals are correlated	Two or more independent variables are correlated
Effect?	Too many Type I errors	Type I errors (for positive correlation)	Too many Type II errors

Model Misspecification

There are six common misspecifications of the regression model that you should be aware of and be able to recognize:

1. Omitting a variable.
2. Transforming variable.

3. Incorrectly pooling data.
4. Using a lagged dependent variable as an independent variable.
5. Forecasting the past.
6. Measuring independent variables with error.

The effects of the model misspecification on the regression results are basically the same for all the misspecifications: regression coefficients are biased and inconsistent, which means we can't have any confidence in our hypothesis tests of the coefficients or in the predictions of the model.

Time-Series Analysis

Cross-Reference to CFA Institute Assigned Topic Review #13

Types of Time Series

Linear Trend Model

The typical time series uses time as the independent variable to estimate the value of time series (the dependent variable) in period *t*:

$$y_t = b_0 + b_1(t) + \varepsilon_t$$

The predicted change in y is b_1 and t = 1, 2, ..., T

Trend models are limited in that they assume time explains the dependent variable. Also, they tend to be plagued by various assumption violations. The Durbin-Watson test statistic can be used to check for serial correlation. A linear trend model may be appropriate if the data points seem to be equally distributed above and below the line and the mean is constant. Growth in GDP and inflation levels are likely candidates for linear models.

Log-Linear Trend Model

Log-linear regression assumes the dependent financial variable grows at some constant rate:

$$y_t = e^{b_0 + b_1(t)}$$

$$\ln(y_t) = \ln(e^{b_0 + b_1(t)}) \Rightarrow \ln(y_t) = b_0 + b_1(t)$$

The log-linear model is best for a data series that exhibits a trend or for which the residuals are correlated or predictable or the mean is non-constant. Most of the data related to investments have some type of trend and thus lend themselves more to a log-linear model. In addition, any data that have seasonality are candidates for a log-linear model. Recall that any exponential growth data call for a log-linear model.

The use of the transformed data produces a linear trend line with a better fit for the data and increases the predictive ability of the model. Because the log-linear model more accurately captures the behavior of the time series, the impact of serial correlation in the error terms is minimized.

Autoregressive (AR) Model

In AR models, the dependent variable is regressed against previous values of itself.

An autoregressive model of order *p* can be represented as:

$$x_t = b_0 + b_1 x_{t-1} + b_2 x_{t-2} + \dots + b_p x_{t-p} + \varepsilon_t$$

There is no longer a distinction between the dependent and independent variables (i.e., *x* is the only variable). An AR(p) model is specified correctly if the autocorrelations of residuals from the model are not statistically significant at any lag.

When testing for serial correlation in an AR model, don't use the Durbin-Watson statistic. Use a *t*-test to determine whether any of the correlations between residuals at any lag are statistically significant.

If some are significant, the model is incorrectly specified and a lagged variable at the indicated lag should be added.

Chain Rule of Forecasting

Multiperiod forecasting with AR models is done one period at a time, where risk increases with each successive forecast because it is based on previously forecasted values. The calculation of successive forecasts in this manner is referred to as the *chain rule of forecasting*. A one-period-ahead forecast for an AR(1) model is determined in the following manner:

$$\hat{x}_{t+1} = \hat{b}_0 + \hat{b}_1 x_t$$

Likewise, a 2-step-ahead forecast for an AR(1) model is calculated as:

$$\hat{x}_{t+2} = \hat{b}_0 + \hat{b}_1 \hat{x}_{t+1}$$

Autocorrelations

One of the assumptions underlying linear regression is that the residuals are uncorrelated with each other. If a time series model's residuals exhibit serial correlation, the model is not appropriate for the time series and we should not use it to predict future performance without making appropriate corrections.

Covariance Stationary

Statistical inferences based on a lagged time series model may be invalid unless we can make the assumption that the time series being modeled is covariance stationary. A time series is covariance stationary if it satisfies the following three conditions:

1. Constant and finite expected value.
2. Constant and finite variance.
3. Constant and finite covariance with leading or lagged values.

To determine whether a time series is covariance stationary, we can:

- Plot the data to see if the mean and variance remain constant (often detects seasonality).
- Run an AR model and test correlations.
- Perform the Dickey-Fuller test (which is a test for a unit root, or if $b_1 - 1$ is equal to zero).

If the times series does not satisfy these conditions, we say it is not covariance stationary, or that there is nonstationarity. Most economic and financial time series relationships are not stationary. The degree of nonstationarity depends on the length of the series and the underlying economic and market environment and conditions.

For an AR(1) model to be covariance stationary, the mean reverting level must be defined. Stated differently, b_1 must be less than one.

If the AR model is not covariance stationary, we can often correct it with first differencing.

Mean Reversion

A time series is mean reverting if it tends towards its mean over time. The mean reverting level for an AR(1) model is $\frac{b_0}{(1-b_1)}$.

The value of the dependent variable tends to fall when above its mean and rise when below its mean.

Unit Root

If the value of the lag coefficient is equal to one, the time series is said to have a unit root and will follow a random walk process. A series with a unit root is not covariance stationary. Economic and finance time series frequently have unit roots. First differencing will often eliminate the unit root. If there is a unit root, this period's value is equal to last period's value plus a random error term and the mean reverting level is undefined.

Random Walk

A random walk time series is one for which the value in one period is equal to the value in another period, plus a random (unpredictable) error. If we believe a time series is a random walk (i.e., has a unit root), we can transform the data to a covariance stationary time series using a procedure called first differencing.

Random walk without a drift: $x_t = x_{t-1} + \varepsilon_t$

Random walk with a drift: $x_t = b_0 + x_{t-1} + \varepsilon_t$

- In either case, the mean reverting level is undefined ($b_1 = 1$), so the series is not covariance stationary.
- Need to use first differencing, and the new dependent variable is the change in *x* from one period to the next.

First Differencing

The first differencing process involves subtracting the value of the time series (i.e., the dependent variable) in the immediately preceding period from the current value of the time series to define a new dependent variable, *y*. If the original time series has a unit root, this means we can define y_t as:

$$y_t = x_t - x_{t-1} \Rightarrow y_t = \varepsilon_t$$

Then, stating *y* in the form of an AR(1) model:

$$y_t = b_0 + b_1 y_{t-1} + \varepsilon_t$$

where:
$b_0 = b_1 = 0$

This transformed time series has a finite mean-reverting level of $\frac{0}{1-0} = 0$ and is, therefore, covariance stationary.

First differencing can remove a trend in the data and result in a covariance stationary series.

Professor's Note: By taking first differences, you model the change in the value of the dependent variable rather than the value of the dependent variable.

Seasonality

Seasonality in a time series is tested by calculating the autocorrelations of error terms. A statistically significant lagged error term may indicate seasonality. To adjust for seasonality in an AR model, an additional lag of the independent variable (corresponding to the statistically significant lagged error term) is added to the original model. Usually, if quarterly data are used, the seasonal lag is 4; if monthly data are used, the seasonal lag is 12. If a seasonal lag coefficient is appropriate and corrects the seasonality, a revised model incorporating the seasonal lag will show no statistical significance of the lagged error terms.

Assessing Forecast Accuracy With Root Mean Squared Error (RMSE)

Root mean squared error (RMSE) is used to assess the predictive accuracy of autoregressive models. For example, you could compare the results of an AR(1) and an AR(2) model. The RMSE is the square root of the average (or mean) squared error. The model with the lower RMSE is better.

Out-of-sample forecasts predict values using a model for periods beyond the time series used to estimate the model. The RMSE of a model's out-of-sample forecasts should be used to compare the accuracy of alternative models.

Structural Change (Coefficient Instability)

Estimated regression coefficients change from one time period to another. There is a trade off between the statistical reliability of a long time series and the stability of a short time series. You need to ask, has the economic process or environment changed?

A structural change is indicated by a significant shift in the plotted data at a point in time that seems to divide the data into two distinct patterns. When this is the case, you have to run two different models, one incorporating the data before and one after that date, and test whether the time series has actually shifted. If the time series has shifted significantly, a single time series encompassing the entire period (i.e., both patterns) will likely produce unreliable results, so the most recent model may be more appropriate.

Cointegration

Cointegration means that two time series are economically linked (related to the same macro variables) or follow the same trend and that relationship is not expected to change. If two time series are cointegrated, the error term from regressing one on the other is covariance stationary and the *t*-tests are reliable.

To test whether two time series are cointegrated, we regress one variable on the other using the following model:

$$y_t = b_0 + b_1 x_t + \varepsilon$$

where:
y_t = value of time series y at time t
x_t = value of time series x at time t

The residuals are tested for a unit root using the Dickey-Fuller test with critical *t*-values calculated by Engle and Granger (i.e., the DF-EG test). If the test *rejects* the null hypothesis of a unit root, we say the error terms generated by the two time series are covariance stationary and the two series are cointegrated. If the two series are cointegrated, we can use the regression to model their relationship.

Occasionally, an analyst will run a regression using two time series (i.e., two time series with different variables). For example, to use the market model to estimate the equity beta for a stock, the analyst regresses a time series of the stock's returns on a time series of returns for the market.

- If both time series are covariance stationary, model is reliable.
- If only the dependent variable time series or only the independent time series is covariance stationary, the model is not reliable.
- If neither time series is covariance stationary, you need to check for cointegration.

Autoregressive Conditional Heteroskedasticity (ARCH)

ARCH describes the condition where the variance of the residuals in one time period within a time series is dependent on the variance of the residuals in another period. When this condition exists, the standard errors of the regression coefficients in AR models and the hypothesis tests of these coefficients are invalid.

The ARCH(1) regression model is expressed as:

$$\hat{\varepsilon}_t^2 = a_0 + a_1\hat{\varepsilon}_{t-1}^2 + \mu_t$$

If the coefficient, a_1, is statistically different from zero, the time series is ARCH(1).

If a time-series model has been determined to contain ARCH errors, regression procedures that correct for heteroskedasticity, such as generalized least squares, must be used in order to develop a predictive model. Otherwise, the standard errors of the model's coefficients will be incorrect, leading to invalid conclusions.

However, if a time series has ARCH errors, an ARCH model can be used to predict the variance of the residuals in following periods. For example, if the data exhibit an ARCH(1) pattern, the ARCH(1) model can be used in period t to predict the variance of the residuals in period t + 1:

$$\hat{\sigma}_{t+1}^2 = \hat{a}_0 + \hat{a}_1\hat{\varepsilon}_t^2$$

Summary: The Time-Series Analysis Process

The following steps provide a summary of the time-series analysis process. Note that you may not need to go through all nine steps. For example, notice that by Step C, if there is no seasonality or structural change and the residuals do not exhibit serial correlation, the model is appropriate.

Step A: Evaluate the investment situation you are analyzing and select a model. If you choose a time series model, follow steps B through I.

Step B: Plot the data and check that it is covariance stationarity. Signs of nonstationarity include linear trend, exponential trends, seasonality, or a structural change in the data.

Step C: If no seasonality or structural change, decide between a linear or log-linear model.
- Calculate the residuals.
- Check for serial correlation using the Durbin-Watson statistic.
- If no serial correlation, model is appropriate to use.

Step D: If you find serial correlation, prepare to use an auto regressive (AR) model by making it covariance stationary. This includes:
- Correcting for a linear trend—use first differencing.
- Correcting for an exponential trend—take natural log and first difference.
- Correcting for a structural shift—estimate the models before and after the change.
- Correcting for seasonality—add a seasonal lag (see Step G).

Step E: After the series is covariance stationary, use an AR(1) model to model the data.
- Test residuals for significant serial correlations.
- If no significant correlation, model is okay to use.

Step F: If the residuals from the AR(1) exhibit serial correlation, use an AR(2) model.
- Test residuals for significant serial correlations.
- If no significant correlation, model is okay to use.
- If significant correlation found, keep adding to the AR model until there is no significant serial correlation.

Step G: Check for seasonality.
- Plot data.
- Check seasonal residuals (autocorrelations) for significance.
- If residuals are significant, add the appropriate lag (e.g., for monthly data, add the 12th lag of the time series).

Step H: Check for ARCH.

Step I: Test the model on out-of-sample data.

Economics

Study Session 4

Topic Weight on Exam	5–10%
SchweserNotes™ Reference	Book 1, Pages 262–343

Economics will most likely be tested by asking you to apply the investment tools you learn in this section to the analysis of equity, fixed income, and derivative securities. For example, the lessons learned from economic growth models can be applied to the credit analysis of sovereign debt in Study Session 14. As you read through the Level II economics material, look for links to security valuation and think about how the concepts might be tested as part of a broader valuation item set.

Currency Exchange Rates: Determination and Forecasting

Cross-Reference to CFA Institute Assigned Topic Review #14

Currency Cross Rates

A *cross rate* is the rate of exchange between two currencies implied by their exchange rates with a common third currency.

Suppose we are given three currencies A, B, and C. We can have three pairs of currencies (i.e., A/B, A/C, and B/C).

Rules:

$$\left(\frac{A}{C}\right)_{bid} = \left(\frac{A}{B}\right)_{bid} \times \left(\frac{B}{C}\right)_{bid}$$

$$\left(\frac{A}{C}\right)_{offer} = \left(\frac{A}{B}\right)_{offer} \times \left(\frac{B}{C}\right)_{offer}$$

To calculate the profits from a *triangular arbitrage*, imagine that three currencies each represent a corner of a triangle. Begin with a first currency (usually given in the question—we call it the home currency) and go around the triangle by exchanging the home currency for the first foreign currency, then exchanging the first foreign currency for the second foreign currency, and then exchanging the second foreign currency back into the home currency. If we end up with more money than we started with, we've earned an arbitrage profit.

The bid-ask spread forces us to buy a currency at a higher rate going one way than we can sell it for going the other way.

Follow the "up-the-bid-and-multiply and down-the-ask-and-divide" rule.

Example: Triangular arbitrage

The following quotes are available from your dealer.

Quotes:
USD/EUR 1.271–1.272
EUR/GBP 1.249–1.250
USD/GBP 1.600–1.601

Is an arbitrage profit possible? If so, compute the arbitrage profit in USD if you start with USD 1 million.

Answer:

The implied cross rates:

$$\left(\frac{\text{USD}}{\text{GBP}}\right)_{\text{bid}} = \left(\frac{\text{USD}}{\text{EUR}}\right)_{\text{bid}} \times \left(\frac{\text{EUR}}{\text{GBP}}\right)_{\text{bid}} = 1.271 \times 1.249 = 1.587$$

$$\left(\frac{\text{USD}}{\text{GBP}}\right)_{\text{ask}} = \left(\frac{\text{USD}}{\text{EUR}}\right)_{\text{ask}} \times \left(\frac{\text{EUR}}{\text{GBP}}\right)_{\text{ask}} = 1.272 \times 1.250 = 1.590$$

Since the dealer quote of USD/GBP = 1.600–1.601 falls outside of these cross rates, arbitrage profit may be possible (i.e., we have to check it).

There are two possible paths around the triangle (we are given the starting position in USD):

Path 1: USD → GBP → EUR → USD

Path 2: USD → EUR → GBP → USD

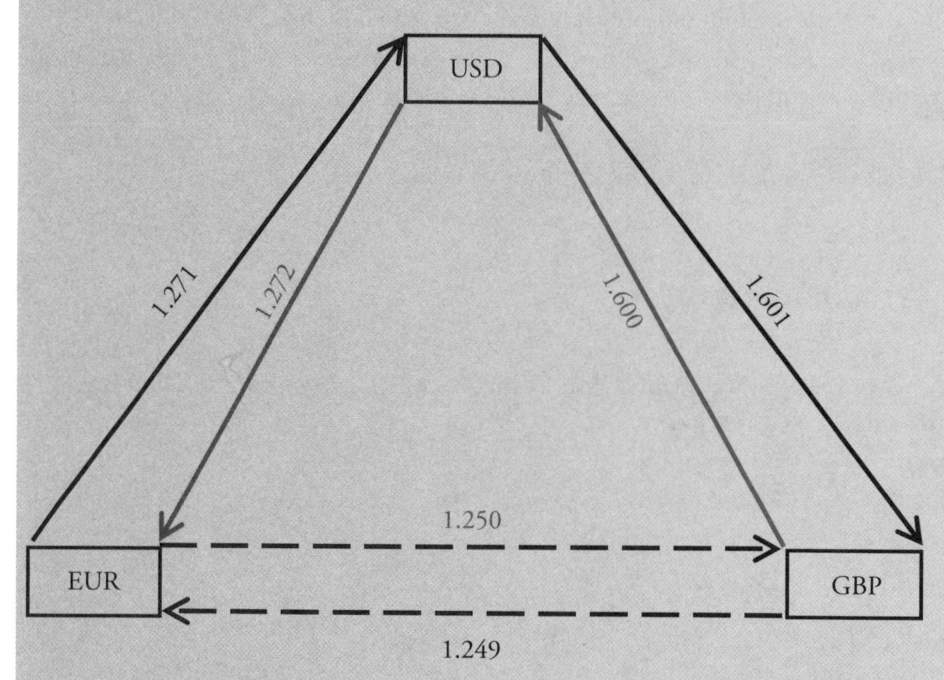

Since the dealer quotes imply that USD is undervalued relative to GBP (it costs more in USD to buy GBP using the dealer quote compared to the implied cross rates), if arbitrage exists, it will be via path 2. Make sure to use dealer quotes in the steps below instead of implied cross rates.

Step 1: Convert 1 million USD into EUR @ 1.272 = EUR 786,164
Step 2: Convert EUR 786,164 into GBP @ 1.250 = GBP 628,931
Step 3: Convert GBP 628,931 into USD @ 1.600 = USD 1,006,289

Arbitrage profit = USD 6,289

Note: In step 1, we are going from USD to EUR ("down" the USD/EUR quote), hence we divide USD 1,000,000 by the ask rate of 1.272. The same logic is used for steps 2 and 3. Note also that we did not have to compute the implied cross rate to solve this problem: we could've simply computed the end result using both paths to see if either would give us an arbitrage profit.

Mark-to-Market Value of a Forward Contract

The *mark-to-market value* of a forward contract reflects the profit that would be realized by closing out the position at current market prices, which is equivalent to offsetting the contract with an equal and opposite forward position:

$$V_t = \frac{(FP_t - FP)(\text{contract size})}{\left[1 + R\left(\frac{\text{days}}{360}\right)\right]}$$

where:

V_t = value of the forward contract at time *t* (to the party buying the base currency), denominated in the price currency.

FP_t = forward price (to sell base currency) at time *t* in the market for a new contract maturing at time *T* ($t < T$).

days = number of days remaining to maturity of the forward contract (T–t).

R = the interest rate of the price currency.

Example: Mark-to-market value of a forward contract

Yew Mun Yip has entered into a 90-day forward contract long CAD 1 million against AUD at a forward rate of 1.05358 AUD/CAD. Thirty days after initiation, the following AUD/CAD quotes are available:

Maturity	FX Rate
Spot	1.0612/1.0614
30-day	+4.9/+5.2
60-day	+8.6/+9.0
90-day	+14.6/+16.8
180-day	+42.3/+48.3

The following information is available (at t=30) for AUD interest rates:

30-day rate: 1.12%

60-day rate: 1.16%

90-day rate: 1.20%

What is the mark-to-market value in AUD of Yip's forward contract?

Answer:

Yip's contract calls for long CAD (i.e., converting AUD to CAD). To value the contract, we would look to unwind the position. To unwind the position, Yip can take an offsetting position in a new forward contract with the same maturity. Hence, Yip would be selling CAD in exchange for AUD and, hence, going up the bid (i.e., use the bid price). Note that after 30 days, 60 more days remain in the original contract.

The forward bid price for a new contract expiring in T – t = 60 days is 1.0612 + 8.6/10,000 = 1.06206.

The interest rate to use for discounting the value is also the 60-day AUD interest rate of 1.16%:

$$V_t = \frac{(FP_t - FP)(\text{contract size})}{\left[1 + R\left(\frac{\text{days}}{360}\right)\right]} = \frac{(1.06206 - 1.05358)(1{,}000{,}000)}{\left[1 + 0.0116\left(\frac{60}{360}\right)\right]} = 8{,}463.64$$

Thirty days into the forward contract, Yip's position has gained (positive value) AUD 8,463.64. This is because Yip's position is long CAD, which has appreciated relative to AUD since inception of the contract. Yip can close out the contract on that day and receive AUD 8,463.64.

Note: Be sure to use the AUD (price currency) interest rate.

International Parity Conditions

Note: Exchange rates (where applicable) below follow the convention of A/B.

Covered interest arbitrage:

Covered interest rate parity holds when any forward premium or discount exactly offsets differences in interest rates so an investor would earn the same return investing in either currency. Covered in this context means it holds by arbitrage.

$$F = \frac{\left(1 + R_A\left(\frac{\text{days}}{360}\right)\right)}{\left(1 + R_B\left(\frac{\text{days}}{360}\right)\right)} S_0$$

Uncovered interest rate parity:

Uncovered interest rate parity relates expected future spot exchange rates (instead of forward exchange rates) to interest rate differentials. Since the expected spot price is not market traded, uncovered interest rate parity does not hold by arbitrage.

$$E(S_t) = \text{expected spot rate at time t} = \left(\frac{1+R_A}{1+R_B}\right)^t (S_0)$$

Comparing covered and uncovered interest parity, we see that covered interest rate parity gives us the no-arbitrage forward exchange rate, while uncovered interest rate parity gives us the *expected* future spot exchange rate (which is not market traded).

International Fisher relation:

$$\frac{(1+R_{\text{nominal A}})}{(1+R_{\text{nominal B}})} = \frac{[1+E(\text{inflation}_A)]}{[1+E(\text{inflation}_B)]}$$

This relation tells us that the difference between two countries' nominal interest rates should be approximately equal to the difference between their expected inflation rates.

Relative purchasing power parity (relative PPP) states that changes in exchange rates should exactly offset the price effects of any inflation differential between two countries.

Relative PPP:

$$S_t = S_0\left[\frac{1+\text{inflation}_A}{1+\text{inflation}_B}\right]^t$$

Figure 1: The International Parity Relationships Combined

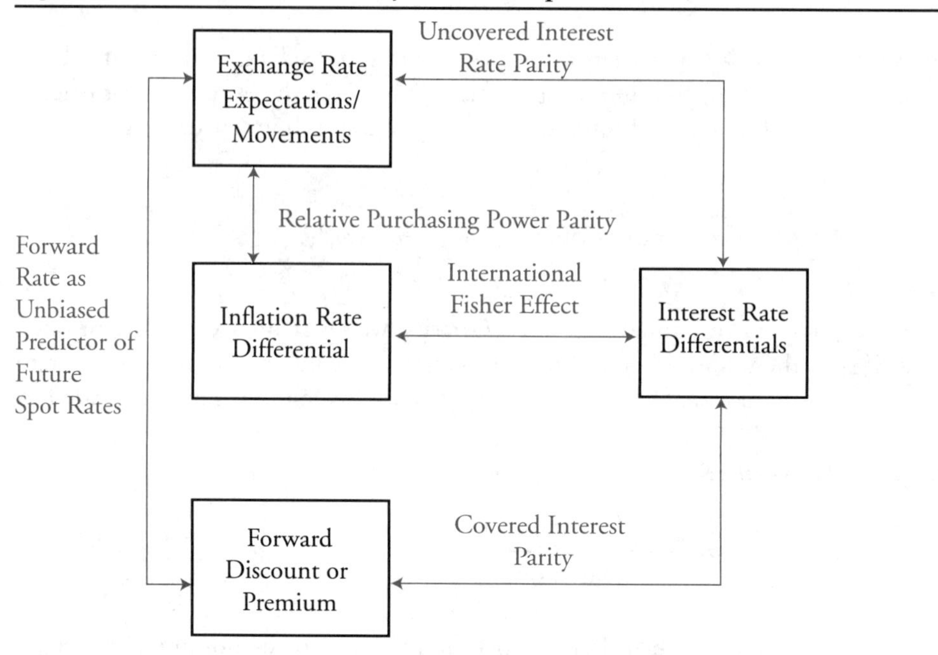

Several observations can be made from the relationships among the various parity relationships:

- Covered interest parity holds by arbitrage. If forward rates are unbiased predictors of future spot rates, uncovered interest rate parity also holds (and vice versa).
- Interest rate differentials should mirror inflation differentials. This holds true if the international Fisher relation holds. If that is true, we can also use inflation differentials to forecast future exchange rates which is the premise of the ex-ante version of PPP.
- By combining relative purchasing power parity with the international Fisher relation, we get uncovered interest rate parity.

Real Exchange Rates

If relative PPP holds at any point in time, the *real exchange rate* will be constant, and is called the equilibrium real exchange rate. However, since relative PPP seldom holds over the short term, the real exchange rate fluctuates around this mean-reverting equilibrium value.

$$\text{real exchange rate (A/B)} = \text{equilibrium real exchange rate} + (\text{real interest rate}_B - \text{real interest rate}_A) - (\text{risk premium}_B - \text{risk premium}_A)$$

Several observations can be made about the relationship identified above:

- This relationship should only be used to assess the direction of change (i.e., appreciate/depreciate) in real exchange rates rather than precise estimates of exchange rates.
- In the short term, the real value of a currency fluctuates around its long-term, equilibrium value.
- The real value of a currency is positively related to its real interest rate and negatively related to the risk premium investors demand for investing in assets denominated in the currency.
- The real interest rate increases when the nominal interest rate increases (keeping inflation expectations unchanged) or when expected inflation decreases (keeping nominal interest rates unchanged).

The FX Carry Trade

The *FX carry trade* seeks to profit from the failure of uncovered interest rate parity to hold in the short run. In an FX carry trade, the investor invests in a high-yield currency while borrowing in a low-yield currency. If the higher yield currency does not depreciate by the interest rate differential, the investor makes a profit.

profit on carry trade
= interest differential – change in the spot rate of investment currency

The carry trade is inherently a leveraged trade that is exposed to crash risk, as the underlying return distributions of carry trades are non-normal (negative skewness and excess kurtosis). Risk management in carry trade may be implemented through a valuation filter or a volatility filter.

Balance of Payments (BOP) Analysis

BOP influence on exchange rates can be analyzed based on current account influence and capital account influence.

Current account influences include:

- *Flow mechanism*: A current account deficit puts downward pressure on the exchange value of a country's currency. The decrease in the value of the currency *may* restore the current account deficit to a balance depending on the initial deficit, the influence of exchange rates on export and import prices, and the price elasticity of demand of traded goods.
- *Portfolio composition mechanism*: Investor countries with capital account deficits (and current account surpluses) may find their portfolios dominated

by investments in countries persistently running capital account surpluses (and current account deficits). If/when the investor countries rebalance their portfolios, the investee countries' currencies may depreciate.

- *Debt sustainability mechanism*: A country running a current account deficit may be running a capital account surplus by borrowing from abroad. When the level of debt gets too high relative to GDP, investors may question the sustainability of this level of debt, leading to a rapid depreciation of the borrower's currency.

Capital account inflows (outflows) are one of the major causes of appreciation (depreciation) of a country's currency.

Approaches to Exchange Rate Determination

1. Mundell-Fleming model

Figure 2 shows the impact of monetary and fiscal policies in the short run under the *Mundell-Fleming model.*

Figure 2: Monetary and Fiscal Policy and Exchange Rates

Monetary Policy/Fiscal Policy	*Capital Mobility*	
	High	*Low*
Expansionary/expansionary	Uncertain	Depreciation
Expansionary/restrictive	Depreciation	Uncertain
Restrictive/expansionary	Appreciation	Uncertain
Restrictive/restrictive	Uncertain	Appreciation

2. Monetary models

The monetary models focus on the influence of monetary policy on inflation and, hence, exchange rates.

A) **Pure monetary model:** PPP holds at any point in time and, therefore, an expansionary monetary policy results in an increase in inflation and a depreciation of the home currency.

B) **Dornbusch overshooting model:** A restrictive (expansionary) monetary policy leads to an appreciation (depreciation) of the domestic currency in the short term and then a slow depreciation (appreciation) toward the long-term PPP value.

3. **Portfolio balance model (asset market approach):** Focuses on the long-term implications of sustained fiscal policy (deficit or surplus) on currency values. When the government runs a fiscal deficit, it borrows money from investors. Under the portfolio balance approach, sustained fiscal deficits will lead to eventual depreciation of the home currency.

Capital Controls and Central Bank Intervention

Capital controls and central bank intervention aim to reduce excessive capital inflows which could lead to speculative bubbles. The success of central bank intervention depends on the size of official FX reserves at the disposal of the central bank relative to the average trading volume in the country's currency. For developed markets, central bank resources on a relative basis are too insignificant to be effective at managing exchange rates. However, some emerging market countries with large FX reserves relative to trading volume have been somewhat effective. Persistent and large capital flows are harder for central banks to manage using capital controls.

Warning Signs of an Impending Currency Crisis

- Terms of trade deteriorate.
- Official foreign exchange reserves dramatically decline.
- Real exchange rate is substantially higher than the mean-reverting level.
- Inflation increases.
- Equity markets experience a boom-bust cycle.
- Money supply relative to bank reserves increases.
- Nominal private credit grows.

Economic Growth and the Investment Decision

Cross-Reference to CFA Institute Assigned Topic Review #15

Preconditions for Economic Growth

The following factors are positively related to growth rate of an economy:

- Level of savings and investment.
- Developed financial markets and intermediaries.
- Political stability, rule of law, and property rights.
- Investment in human capital (e.g., education, health care).
- Favorable tax and regulatory systems.
- Free trade and unrestricted capital flows.

Sustainable Growth Rate of an Economy

In the long run, the rate of aggregate stock market appreciation is limited to the sustainable growth rate of the economy.

Potential GDP

Potential GDP represents the maximum output of an economy without putting upward pressure on prices. Higher potential GDP growth increases the potential for stock returns and also increases the credit quality of fixed income investments.

In the short term, the difference between potential GDP and actual GDP may be useful for predicting fiscal/monetary policy. If actual GDP is less than potential GDP, inflation is unlikely and the government may follow an expansionary policy.

Capital Deepening Investment and Technological Process

Cobb-Douglas Production Function

$$Y = TK^{\alpha}L^{(1-\alpha)}$$

where:
Y = the level of aggregate output in the economy
α and $(1 - \alpha)$ = the share of output allocated to capital (K) and labor (L), respectively
T = a scale factor that represents the technological progress of the economy, often referred to as *total factor productivity* (TFP)

The *Cobb-Douglas function* essentially states that output (GDP) is a function of labor and capital inputs, and their productivity. It exhibits constant returns to scale; increasing all inputs by a fixed percentage leads to the same percentage increase in output.

Dividing both sides by L in the Cobb-Douglas production function, we can obtain the output per worker (labor productivity).

$$\text{output per worker} = Y/L = T(K/L)^{\alpha}$$

Capital deepening is an increase in the capital stock and the capital-to-labor ratio. Due to diminishing marginal product of capital, increases in the capital stock can lead to only limited increases in output and labor productivity if the capital-to-labor ratio is already high.

Technological progress impacts the productivity of all inputs—labor and capital. The long-term growth rate can be increased by technological progress (also called *total factor productivity*) since output and labor efficiency are increased at all levels of capital-to-labor ratios.

In steady state (i.e., equilibrium), the marginal product of capital ($MPK = \alpha Y/K$) and marginal cost of capital (i.e., the *rental price of capital*, r) are equal, hence $\alpha Y/K = r$.

The productivity curves in Figure 3 show the effect of increasing capital per worker on output per worker. Capital deepening is a movement *along* the productivity curve. The curvature of the relationship derives from the diminishing marginal productivity of capital. Technological progress *shifts* the productivity curve upward and will lead to increased productivity at all levels of capital per worker.

Figure 3: Productivity Curves

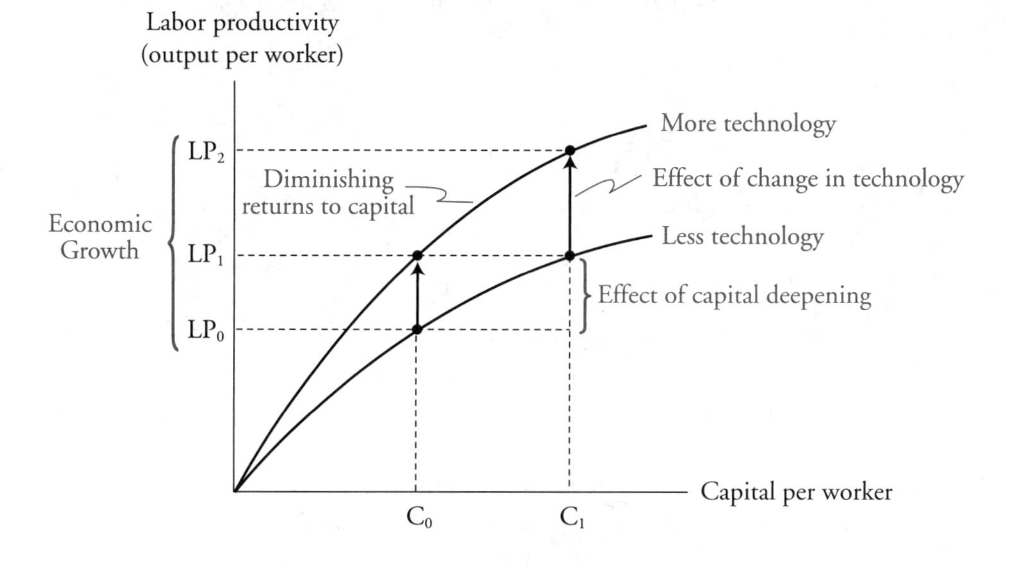

Growth Accounting Relations

growth rate in potential GDP = long-term growth rate of technology + α (long-term growth rate in capital) + $(1-\alpha)$ (long-term growth rate in labor)

or

growth rate in potential GDP = long-term growth rate of labor force + long-term growth rate in labor productivity

Example: Estimating potential GDP growth rate

Azikland is an emerging market economy where labor accounts for 60% of total factor cost. The long-term trend of labor growth of 1.5% is expected to continue. Capital investment has been growing at 3%. The country has benefited greatly from borrowing the technology of more developed countries; total factor productivity is expected to increase by 2% annually. **Compute** the potential GDP growth rate for Azikland.

Answer:

Using the growth accounting equation,

$$\%\Delta Y = 2\% + (0.4)(3\%) + (0.6)(1.5\%) = 4.1\%$$

Theories of Economic Growth

Classical growth theory contends that growth in real GDP per capita is temporary—when the GDP per capita rises above the subsistence level, a population explosion occurs and GDP per capita is driven back to the subsistence level.

Neoclassical growth theory contends that the sustainable growth rate of an economy is a function of population growth, labor's share of income, and the rate of technological advancement. Growth gains from other means, such as increased savings, are only temporary.

Under the neoclassical growth theory, *sustainable growth of output per capita* (g^*) is equal to growth rate in technology (θ) divided by labor's share of GDP ($1-\alpha$):

$$g^* = \frac{\theta}{(1-\alpha)}$$

The sustainable growth rate of output (G^*) is equal to the sustainable growth rate of output per capita plus growth of labor (ΔL).

Neoclassical theory yields several implications about sustainable growth and inputs:

- Capital deepening affects the level of output but not the growth rate in the long run. Capital deepening may lead to temporary growth but growth will revert back to the sustainable level if there is no change in technology.
- The growth rate in an economy will move toward its steady state rate regardless of initial capital to labor ratio or level of technology.
- In the long term, the growth rate in productivity (i.e., output per capita) is a function of only the growth rate of technology (θ) and the share of labor to total output ($1-\alpha$).
- Capital deepening may lead to temporary growth but growth will revert back to the sustainable level if there is no change in technology.
- An increase in savings will only temporarily raise the rate of growth in an economy. However, countries with a higher savings rate will enjoy a higher capital to labor ratio and higher productivity.

Endogenous growth theory acknowledges the impact of technological progress within the model. Under endogenous growth theory, investment in capital can have constant returns, unlike neoclassical theory which assumes diminishing returns to capital. This assumption allows for a permanent increase in growth rate attributable to an increase in savings rate. Research and development expenditures are often cited as examples of capital investment that increase technological progress.

Convergence Hypotheses

The **absolute convergence** hypothesis states that less-developed countries will converge to the standard of living of developed countries.

The **conditional convergence** hypothesis assumes that convergence in living standards will occur for countries with the same savings rate, population growth, and production functions.

The **club convergence** hypothesis contends that some less developed countries may converge to developed standards if they are in the "club" of countries. A club comprises countries with similar institutional structures, such as property rights and political stability. Countries outside of the club (without the appropriate institutional structures) will not converge.

Economics of Regulation

Cross-Reference to CFA Institute Assigned Topic Review #16

Regulations and Regulators

Regulations can be classified as:

- *Statutes* (laws made by legislative bodies).
- *Administrative regulations* (rules issued by government agencies or other bodies authorized by the government).
- *Judicial law* (findings of courts).

Regulators can be government agencies or independent regulators. *Independent regulators* can either be *self-regulatory organizations* (SROs) or non-SROs. Additionally, there are *outside bodies* like FASB that are not regulators themselves, but their output (standards in the case of FASB) are referenced by regulators.

Figure 4: Type of Regulators

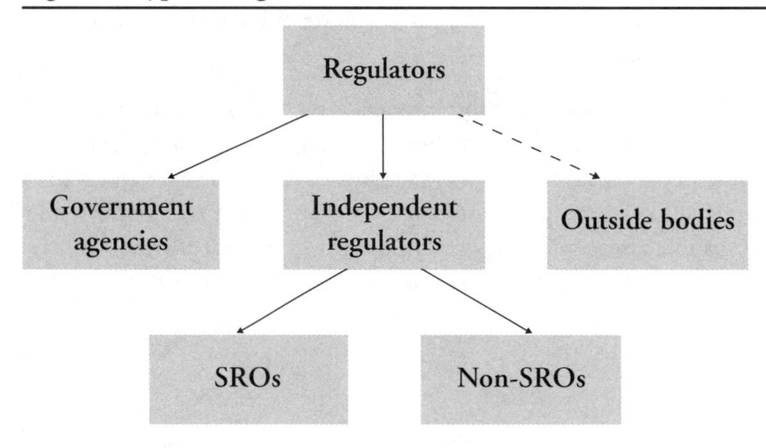

SROs without government recognition are not considered regulators. Self-regulating organizations, while independent of the government and relatively immune from political pressure, may still be subject to pressure from their members. Independent SROs—when properly supervised by regulatory agencies—have been effective in carrying out the objectives of the regulation.

Economic Rationale for Regulation

Regulations are needed in the presence of:

- *Informational frictions*, when information is not equally available or distributed.
- *Externalities*, which deal with the consumption of public goods wherein cost is not proportional to consumption.

Regulatory Interdependencies

The **regulatory capture** theory states that a regulatory body will eventually be influenced or even controlled by the industry that is it is supposed to regulate. Regulatory differences between jurisdictions can lead to *regulatory competition* wherein regulators compete to provide the most attractive regulatory environment. Firms may take advantage of **regulatory arbitrage** to exploit the difference between the substance and interpretation of a regulation or the differences between regulations in different countries.

Regulatory Tools

Tools of regulatory intervention include price mechanisms (taxes or subsidies), restrictions on or requirement of certain activities (e.g., banning use of certain chemicals or requiring the filing of financial reports), the provision of public goods (such as roads), and financing of private projects (e.g., funding organizations that are beneficial to society).

Cost/Benefit Analysis of Regulations

Regulatory burden refers to the cost of compliance for the entity being regulated. Regulatory burden minus the private benefits of regulation is known as the *net regulatory burden.* Indirect costs of regulations need to be included in the cost-benefit analysis, but are difficult to measure ex-ante. *Sunset clauses* require a cost-benefit analysis to be revisited before the associated regulation is renewed.

Financial Reporting and Analysis

Study Sessions 5, 6, & 7

Topic Weight on Exam	15–25%
SchweserNotes™ Reference	Book 2, Pages 10–225

Inventory Cost Flow Method

Cross-Reference to CFA Institute Assigned Topic Review #17

The choice of inventory cost flow method (known as the cost flow assumption under U.S. GAAP and cost formula under IFRS) affects the firm's income statement, balance sheet, and many financial ratios. Additionally, the cost flow method can affect the firm's income taxes and, thus, the firm's cash flow. Cost of goods sold (COGS) is related to the beginning balance of inventory, purchases, and the ending balance of inventory.

COGS = beginning inventory + purchases – ending inventory

Notice that the COGS and ending inventory are inversely related. In other words, if a particular valuation method increases the value of ending inventory, the COGS would be lower under that method.

Inventory cost flow methods:

1. FIFO: The cost of the first item purchased is the cost of the first item sold. Ending inventory is based on the cost of the most recent purchases, thereby approximating current cost.

2. LIFO: The cost of the last item purchased is the cost of the first item sold. Ending inventory is based on the cost of the earliest items purchased. Assuming inflation, ending inventory is smaller and COGS is larger compared to those calculated using FIFO. Higher COGS results in lower taxes and, thus, higher cash flow. LIFO is prohibited under IFRS.

3. Weighted average cost: COGS and inventory values are between their FIFO and LIFO values.

4. Specific identification: Each unit sold is matched with the unit's actual cost.

LIFO Reserve

The LIFO reserve is the difference in LIFO ending inventory and FIFO ending inventory. It is used to adjust the LIFO firm's ending inventory and COGS back to FIFO for comparison purposes. To adjust a LIFO firm's financial statements to reflect the FIFO cost flow method:

1. Add the LIFO reserve to current assets (ending inventory).

2. Subtract the income taxes on the LIFO reserve from current assets (cash).

3. Add the LIFO reserve, net of tax, to shareholders' equity.

4. Subtract the *change* in the LIFO reserve from COGS.

5. Add the income taxes on the *change* in the LIFO reserve to income tax expense.

LIFO Liquidation

A LIFO liquidation occurs when a firm sells more inventory than it replaces. The result (in a typical inflationary environment) is lower COGS and higher profit. However, the increase in profit is not sustainable once the current inventory is depleted.

Results of Choice of Method

The choice of method affects numerous financial statement line items and their related financial ratios. Assuming price increases (i.e., inflation) and stable or increasing inventory quantities:

LIFO results in...	*FIFO results in...*
higher COGS	lower COGS
lower taxes	higher taxes
lower net income	higher net income
lower inventory balances	higher inventory balances
lower working capital	higher working capital
higher cash flows (less taxes)	lower cash flows (more taxes)
lower net and gross margins	higher net and gross margins
lower current ratio	higher current ratio
higher inventory turnover	lower inventory turnover
higher debt-to-equity	lower debt-to-equity

Inventory Valuation

Under IFRS, inventories are valued at the lower of cost or net realizable value. Inventory "write-ups" are allowed, but only to the extent that a previous write-down to net realizable value was recorded.

Under U.S. GAAP, inventories are valued at the lower of cost or market. Market is usually equal to replacement cost but cannot exceed net realizable value or be less than net realizable value minus a normal profit margin. No subsequent "write-up" is allowed.

Inventory Analysis

An increase in raw materials and/or work-in-process inventory may be an indication of an expected increase in demand. Conversely, an increase in finished goods inventory, while raw materials and work-in-process are decreasing, may be an indication of decreasing demand. Finished goods inventory that is growing faster than sales may be an indication of declining demand and, ultimately, excessive and potentially obsolete inventory.

The Capitalizing vs. Expensing Decision

Cross-Reference to CFA Institute Assigned Topic Review #18

When a firm makes an expenditure, it can either capitalize the cost as an asset on the balance sheet or expense the cost in the income statement. Capitalizing results in higher assets, higher equity, and higher operating cash flow as compared to expensing. Capitalizing also results in higher earnings in the first year and lower earnings in subsequent years as the capitalized cost is depreciated.

Depreciation Methods

In the early years of an asset's life, accelerated depreciation will result in higher depreciation expense, lower net income, and lower ROA and ROE as compared to straight-line depreciation. Cash flow is the same assuming tax depreciation is unaffected by the choice of method for financial reporting purposes. Firms can lower depreciation expense and increase net income by using longer useful lives and higher salvage values.

Impairment

Under IFRS, an asset is impaired when its carrying value exceeds the recoverable amount. The recoverable amount is the greater of fair value less selling costs and the value in use (present value of expected cash flows). If impaired, the asset is written-down to the recoverable amount. Loss recoveries are permitted. Under U.S. GAAP, an asset is impaired if its carrying value is greater than the asset's undiscounted future cash flows. If impaired, the asset is written-down to fair value. Subsequent recoveries are not allowed for assets held for use.

Asset impairments involve considerable management discretion. When the impairment loss is recognized, ROA and ROE will decrease. In subsequent periods, ROA and ROE will increase as a result of lower assets and lower equity. Impairments have no impact on cash flow. Under IFRS, firms have the option to revalue assets based on fair value. Revaluation under U.S. GAAP is not permitted.

Average Age of Fixed Assets

The average age of fixed assets can be compared to the average useful life to estimate the timing of a company's future capital expenditures.

- Average age (in years) = accumulated depreciation / annual depreciation expense.
- Average depreciable life = ending gross investment / annual depreciation expense.
- Remaining useful life = ending net investment / annual depreciation expense.

Finance and Operating Leases

A finance lease is, in substance, a purchase of an asset that is financed with debt. Finance lease expense consists of depreciation of the asset and interest on the loan. The finance lease payment consists of an operating outflow of cash (interest expense) and a financing outflow of cash (principal reduction). An operating lease is simply a rental arrangement. No asset or liability is reported by the lessee. The rental payment is reported as an expense and as an operating outflow of cash.

Compared to an operating lease, a finance lease will result in higher assets, liabilities, leverage ratios, operating cash flow, and operating income. A finance lease will result in lower net income in the early years of the lease, lower financing cash flows, and lower working capital and current ratio.

Intercorporate Investments

Cross-Reference to CFA Institute Assigned Topic Review #19

Accounting for Intercorporate Investments

Percentage of ownership is typically used as a practical guide to determine influence or control for financial reporting purposes. Figure 1 contains the guidelines used to determine which reporting method is required for intercorporate investments. The conceptual distinction for determining reporting methods centers on the degree to which the investee (affiliate) is an integral part of the investor (parent).

Figure 1: Accounting Standards for Intercorporate Investments

Ownership	*Degree of Influence/Control*	*U.S. GAAP Method*	*IFRS Method*
Less than 20%	No significant influence	Depends on security classification	Same as U.S. GAAP
20% to 50%	Significant influence	Equity method	Same as U.S. GAAP
Each party owns 50%	Shared control	Equity method	Choice of equity method or proportionate consolidation
More than 50%	Control	Acquisition	Same as U.S. GAAP

Classifications of Financial Securities

- *Debt securities held-to-maturity* are securities of which a company has the positive *intent and ability* to hold to maturity. This classification applies only to debt securities; it does not apply to equity investments.
- *Debt and equity securities available-for-sale* may be sold to address the liquidity and other needs of a company.
- *Debt and equity trading securities* are securities acquired for the purpose of selling them in the near term.

Important financial statement effects of the classifications are summarized in Figure 2.

Figure 2: Accounting Treatment for Financial Securities Under U.S. GAAP and IFRS

Classification	*Management Intent*	*U.S. GAAP Balance Sheet Treatment*	*U.S. GAAP Income Statement Treatment*	*Difference Between U.S. GAAP and IFRS*
Trading securities	Acquired for the purpose of selling in the near-term.	Reported at fair market value.	Interest, dividends, realized and unrealized gains and losses reported.	No difference between U.S. GAAP and IFRS.
Available-for-sale securities	May be sold to address liquidity needs.	Reported at fair market value with unrealized gains and losses in comprehensive income in shareholders' equity.	Interest, dividends, and realized gains and losses reported.	Similar to U.S. GAAP, except unrealized foreign exchange gains/ losses which are recognized in the income statement under IFRS.
Held-to-maturity debt securities	Management has positive intent and ability to hold to maturity.	Reported at historical cost.	Interest and any realized gains and losses reported.	No difference between U.S. GAAP and IFRS.

Equity Method

Under the *equity method*, the investment is listed at cost on the balance sheet. Dividends that are paid by the investee increase cash and decrease the investment account on the asset side of the balance sheet. In addition, the investor's pro rata share of the investee's net income increases the asset account and is listed as income on the investor's income statement.

Acquisition Method

Under the acquisition method, the balance sheets of the two entities are *consolidated* as follows: add together all asset and liability accounts net of intercorporate transfers; do not adjust the equity accounts of the parent; and list the minority interest as a separate component of stockholders' equity. Minority interest is equal to the proportion of the subsidiary that the parent does not own times the net equity of the subsidiary.

On the consolidated income statement, add the revenues and expenses of the parent and the subsidiary together as of the consolidation date. Subtract the minority shareholders' share of the subsidiary's net income from this amount. The minority interest amount on the income statement equals the proportion of the subsidiary the parent does not own multiplied by the net income of the subsidiary.

Proportionate Consolidation

A proportionate consolidation is not a provision of U.S. GAAP, although it has been adopted for use under IFRS. Analysts may employ proportionate consolidation on a firm that is currently accounted for using the equity method if the analysts believe that a stronger link exists between the two firms than is implied by the ownership percentage.

A joint venture is a typical example in which you would most likely apply a proportionate consolidation. Proportionate consolidation accounting for joint ventures provides better information to users of financial statements.

When reporting using the proportionate consolidation method, the parent company's share of each asset and liability of the joint venture is included. Only stockholder's equity will be the same under the proportionate consolidation and equity methods. The parent will also include its share of the joint venture's revenues and expenses in its income statement. Net income will not be affected, but many financial ratios will change.

Effect of Choice of Method on Reported Financial Performance

There are four important effects on certain balance sheet and income statement items that result from the choice of accounting method (in most situations):

1. All three methods report the same net income.
2. Equity and proportionate consolidation report the same equity. Acquisition method equity will be higher by the amount of minority interest.
3. Assets and liabilities are highest under the acquisition method and lowest under the equity method; proportionate consolidation is between those two.
4. Sales are highest under the acquisition method and lowest under the equity method; proportionate consolidation is somewhere in between.

Assuming net income is positive, these effects generally result in the equity method reporting the most favorable results, acquisition the least favorable, with proportionate consolidation somewhere in between, as shown in Figure 3.

Figure 3: Differences in Reported Financial Results from Choice of Method

	Equity Method	*Proportionate Consolidation*	*Acquisition*
Leverage	Lower (more favorable) because liabilities are lower and equity is the same.	In between	Higher**
Net profit margin*	Higher because sales are lower and net income is the same.	In between	Lower
ROE	Higher	Same as equity method	Lower
ROA	Higher because net income is the same and assets are lower.	In between	Lower

*Assuming net income is positive.
**Due to inclusion of full liabilities of subsidiary as well as minority interest in equity, the effect on leverage under aquisition method depends on the leverage of the subsidiary.

Special Purpose Entities and Variable Interest Entities

A special purpose entity (SPE), also known as a special purchase vehicle or off-balance sheet entity, is a legal structure created to isolate certain assets and obligations of the sponsor. SPEs are usually formed to serve a specific purpose, so they are limited in scope. The typical motivation is to obtain low-cost financing. An SPE can take the form of a corporation, partnership, joint venture, or trust, although the entity does not necessarily have separate management or even employees.

The Financial Accounting Standards Board (FASB) coined the name variable interest entity (VIE) to identify an SPE that meets certain conditions set forth in FASB interpretation No. 46(R), "Consolidation of Variable Interest Entities" (FIN 46R). If an entity is considered a VIE under FIN 46(R), it must be consolidated by the primary beneficiary. According to FIN 46(R), a variable interest is a contractual, ownership, or other pecuniary interest in an entity that changes as a result of the fair value of the entity's net assets. The variable interest will absorb portions of the SPE's potential losses and receive portions of the potential residual returns.

Following are some examples of common variable interests and the potential risks and residual rewards:

- *At-risk equity investment.* The investor receives the residual benefits but also absorbs the potential losses.
- *Debt guarantee.* In the event of default, the guarantor will experience a loss.

- *Subordinated debt.* Since senior debt is repaid before subordinated debt, the subordinated debtholders absorb the loss in the event the senior debtholders cannot be repaid.
- *Lease residual guarantee.* The lessee guarantees the fair value of the asset at the end of the lease. If the fair value is less than the guaranteed amount, the lessee experiences a loss.
- *Participation rights.* The holder receives a predetermined share of the profit.
- *Asset purchase option.* The holder benefits from an increase in the fair value of the asset.

Consolidation Requirements

Figure 4 summarizes the conditions that identify a VIE.

Figure 4: Is an Entity a VIE?

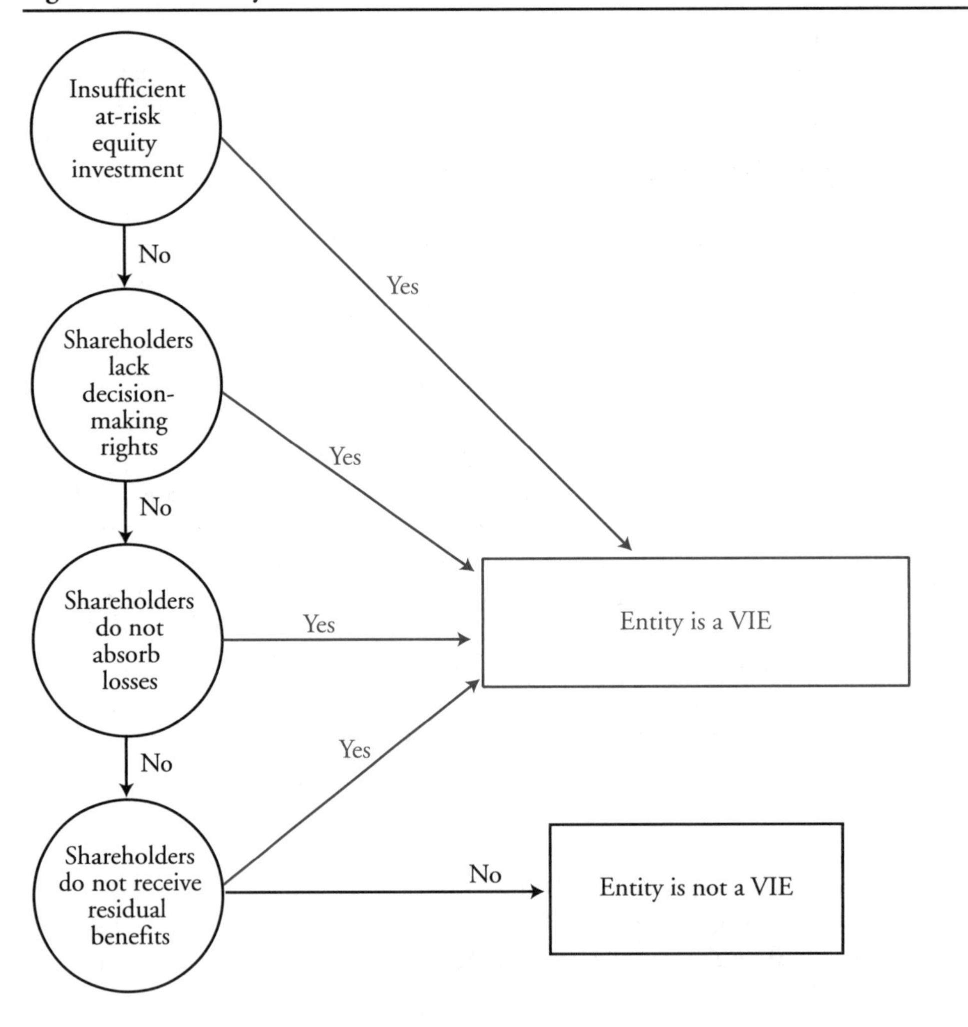

Once it is determined that an entity is a VIE, the entity must be consolidated. The firm that must consolidate the VIE is known as the primary beneficiary. The **primary beneficiary** is the entity that is exposed to the majority of the loss risks or receives the majority of the residual benefits, or both. Voting control is inconsequential at this point.

Employee Compensation: Post-Employment and Share-Based

Cross-Reference to CFA Institute Assigned Topic Review #20

The Pension Obligation for a Defined-Benefit Plan

The **projected benefit obligation** (PBO) is the actuarial present value (at the assumed discount rate) of all future pension benefits earned to date, based on expected future salary increases. It measures the value of the obligation assuming the firm is a going concern.

Reconciliation of Beginning and Ending PBO

Figure 5: Funded Status of a Pension Plan

Plan Assets	PBO
Fair value at the beginning of the year	PBO at the beginning of the year
(+) Contributions	(+) Service cost
(+) Actual return	(+) Interest cost
(–) Benefits paid	(+) Past service cost (plan amendments during the year)
= Fair value at the end of the year	(+/–) Actuarial losses/gains during the year
	(–) Benefits paid
	= PBO at the end of the year

Difference is funded status of the plan:
Plan assets > PBO → Overfunded plan
Plan assets < PBO → Underfunded plan

Balance Sheet Effects

The funded status reflects the economic standing of a pension plan:

funded status = fair value of plan assets – PBO

The balance sheet presentation under both U.S. GAAP and IFRS is as follows:

balance sheet asset (liability) = funded status

Pension Expense Components

Figure 6: Difference Between Recognition of Components of Pension Costs Under U.S. GAAP and IFRS

Component	*U.S. GAAP*	*IFRS*
Current service cost	Income statement	Income statement
Past service cost	OCI, amortized over service life	Income statement
Interest cost	Income statement	Income statement
Expected return	Income statement	Income statement
Actuarial gains/losses	Amortized portion in income statement. Unamortized in OCI.	All in OCI—not amortized (called 'Remeasurements')

Additional explanation for these components follows:

- *Service cost:* increase in the PBO reflecting the pension benefits earned during the year.
- *Interest cost:* increase in PBO resulting from interest owed on the current benefit obligation.
- *Expected return on plan assets:* Under U.S. GAAP, assumed long run rate of return on plan assets used to smooth the volatility that would be caused by using actual returns. Under IFRS, expected rate of return on plan assets is implicitly equal to the discount rate used for computing PBO.
- *Amortization of unrecognized prior service cost:* amortized costs for changes in the PBO that result from amendments to the plan (under U.S. GAAP only). Under IFRS, prior service costs are expensed immediately and not amortized.
- *Amortization and deferral of gains or losses:* amortization of gains and losses caused by (1) changes in actuarial assumptions and (2) differences between actual and expected return on plan assets. Under U.S. GAAP, actuarial gains and losses are recognized in OCI and amortized using the corridor method. Under IFRS, actuarial gains and losses are recognized in OCI and not amortized.

Total Periodic Pension Cost

Analysts often calculate **total periodic pension cost** (TPPC) by eliminating the smoothing amounts and including the *actual* return on assets. The result is a more volatile measure of pension expense. TPPC includes pension expense recognized in the income statement and pension cost that bypasses income statement (i.e., recognized in OCI).

TPPC can be calculated by computing increase in PBO for the period (adjusted for benefits payments) and then subtracting the actual return on assets.

TPPC = ending PBO – beginning PBO + benefits paid – actual return on plan assets

Alternatively, TPPC is equal to the contributions minus the change in funded status during the year.

TPPC = contributions – (ending funded status – beginning funded status)

Fundamental Pension Assumptions

The company must make and disclose three actuarial assumptions in the pension footnotes:

1. The **discount rate** is the interest rate used to compute the present value of the pension obligations. This is the interest rate at which the company could settle its pension obligation. Notice that this is not the risk-free rate.

2. The **rate of compensation increase** is the average annual rate at which employee compensation is expected to increase over time.

3. The **expected return on plan assets** (U.S. GAAP only) is the long-term assumed rate of return on the investments in the plan. Using an expected long-run return assumption rather than actual returns serves to smooth the net pension expense calculation.

Any changes in assumptions that might cause only a small change in the total pension obligation itself can still have a large impact on the net pension asset or liability. The same is true with pension expense; because it is a net amount (service and interest cost net of expected return on plan assets), relatively minor changes in the assumptions can have a major impact on reported pension expense.

Assumptions of high discount rates, low compensation growth rates, and high expected rates of return on plan assets will decrease pension expense, increase earnings, and reduce the pension liability. The more aggressive these assumptions are, the lower the earnings quality of the firm.

The use of a lower rate of compensation growth will improve reported results because it will result in the following:

- Lower estimated future pension payments and, hence, a lower PBO.
- Lower service cost and a lower interest cost; thus, pension expense will decrease.

Figure 7: Effect of Changes in Assumptions

Effect on...	*Increase Discount Rate*	*Decrease Rate of Compensation Increase*	*Increase Expected Rate of Return***
PBO	Decrease	Decrease	No effect
Service cost	Decrease	Decrease	No effect
Interest cost	Decrease*	Decrease	No effect
Pension expense	Decrease*	Decrease	Decrease

* For mature plans, a higher discount rate might increase interest costs. In rare cases, interest cost will increase by enough to offset the decrease in the service cost, and pension expense will increase.
**U.S. GAAP only

Non-Pension Postretirement Benefits

Accounting for *non-pension* postretirement benefits is very similar to accounting for pension benefits, with the following differences:

- The accumulated postretirement benefit obligation (APBO) is the actuarial present value of the expected postretirement benefits. It is estimated using a discount rate applied specifically to those benefits.
- Many postretirement benefit plans are unfunded, which means there are no plan assets, employer contributions equal benefits paid, and the funded status equals the APBO.

Share-Based Compensation

This topic review provides a brief discussion of the key features of the latest standard on accounting for stock-based compensation plans. The key result is that firms must now report compensation expense related to stock option plans on the income statement based on the option's value at issuance. This can significantly decrease reported earnings.

According to SFAS No. 123(R), firms are required to recognize compensation expense based on the fair value of share-based awards as of the grant date. The fair value is estimated using an option pricing model. This expense is amortized over the period required for vesting of the options (i.e., the service period).

Multinational Operations

Cross-Reference to CFA Institute Assigned Topic Review #21

From a financial statement analysis view, there are two tasks that must be understood in multinational operations. First, you must know and be able to apply two different methods of consolidating foreign subsidiaries' operating results into the parent's financial statements. Second, you must understand how these two different accounting procedures affect the parent's financial statements and ratios.

The two methods of consolidation are the *temporal method* (sometimes also referred to as *remeasurement*) and the *current rate method* (a.k.a. *translation*). The appropriate method depends on the subsidiary's functional currency (i.e., the currency in which the subsidiary generates and expends most of its cash). The rules that govern the determination of the functional currency under SFAS 52 are as follows:

- The results of operations, financial position, and cash flows of all foreign operations must be measured in the designated functional currency.
- Self-contained, independent subsidiaries whose operations are primarily located in the local market will use the local currency as the functional currency.
- Subsidiaries whose operations are well integrated with the parent will use the parent's currency as the functional currency.
- If the subsidiary operates in a highly inflationary environment, the parent's currency is the functional currency. A high-inflation environment is defined as one in which cumulative inflation exceeds 100% over a 3-year period.
- If the functional currency is the local currency, use the current rate method.
- If the functional currency is the parent's currency or some other currency, use the temporal method.

Figure 8: Three Methods for Remeasurement/Translation of Local Currencies

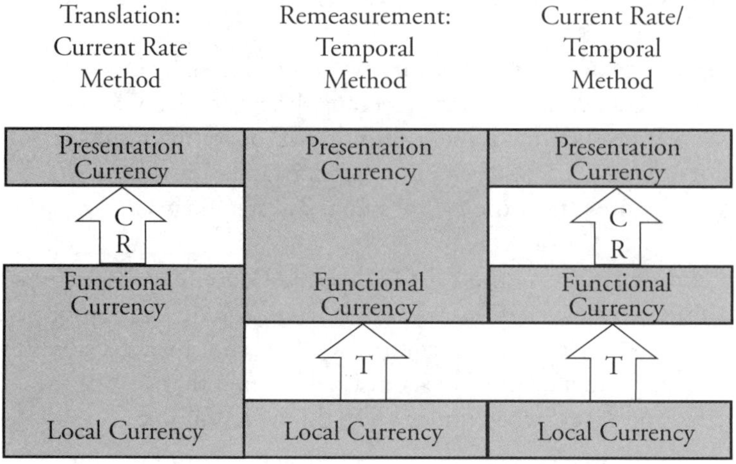

Translation: Current Rate Method	Remeasurement: Temporal Method	Current Rate/ Temporal Method
Presentation Currency	Presentation Currency	Presentation Currency
C R		C R
Functional Currency	Functional Currency	Functional Currency
	T	T
Local Currency	Local Currency	Local Currency

When consolidating the results of foreign subsidiaries, it is important to decide which exchange rate should be used for each account. There are essentially three choices: (1) the current exchange rate, (2) the average exchange rate over the reporting period, and (3) the historical exchange rate (which is the rate that existed when a particular transaction occurred). Which you use depends on which method is appropriate. Study and memorize the information contained in Figure 7.

Figure 9: Exchange Rate Usage Under the Temporal and Current Rate Methods

Account	*Rate Used to Translate Account Using the…*	
	Temporal Method	*Current Rate Method*
Monetary assets/liabilities	Current rate	Current rate
Nonmonetary assets/liabilities	Historical rate	Current rate
Common stock	Historical rate	Historical rate
Equity (taken as a whole)	Mixed*	Current rate**
Revenues and SG&A	Average rate	Average rate
Cost of good sold	Historical rate	Average rate
Depreciation	Historical rate	Average rate
Net income	Mixed*	Average rate
Exposure	Net monetary assets	Shareholders' equity
Exchange rate gain or loss	Income statement	Equity

* Net income is a "mixed rate" under the temporal method because (1) the FX translation gain or loss is shown on the income statement, (2) revenues and SG&A are remeasured at average, while (3) COGS and depreciation are remeasured at historical. Equity is "mixed" because the change in retained earnings (which includes net income) is posted to the equity accounts.

** Under the current rate method, total assets and liabilities are translated at the current rate. The total equity (equity taken as a whole) would then have to be translated at the current rate for the balance sheet to balance.

Calculating the Translation Gain or Loss

Translation gains or losses result from gains or losses related to balance sheet accounts that are translated at the current rate (i.e., they are exposed to changes in exchange rates).

Under the current rate method, all assets and liabilities are translated at the current rate, so the net exposure is assets minus liabilities, or total shareholders' equity:

exposure under the current rate method = shareholders' equity

Under the temporal method, only cash, accounts receivable, accounts payable, current debt, and long-term debt are translated at the current rate (remember that inventory and fixed assets are translated at the historical rate):

exposure under the temporal method = (cash + accounts receivable)
– (accounts payable + current debt + long-term debt) = net monetary assets

Under the current rate method, the translation gains/losses are accumulated on the balance sheet in the equity section as part of comprehensive income in an account called the **cumulative translation adjustment** (CTA).

Under the temporal method, no CTA is reported in shareholders' equity. Instead, the remeasurement gain or loss is recognized in the income statement.

Comparing Subsidiary Results to Translated Results (Current Rate Method)

On the exam, remember these key points regarding the original versus the translated financial statements and ratios.

- Pure balance sheet and pure income statement ratios will be the same.
- If the LC is depreciating, translated mixed ratios (with an income statement item in the numerator and an end-of-period balance sheet item in the denominator) will be larger than the original ratio.
- If the LC is appreciating, translated mixed ratios (with an income statement item in the numerator and an end-of-period balance sheet item in the denominator) will be smaller than the original ratio.

Comparing Results Using the Temporal and Current Rate Methods

The effects on a selected set of ratios of the choice between the current rate and temporal methods are shown in Figure 8.

Figure 10: Effect of Translation Methods on Selected Financial Ratios

	Appreciating Local Currency		Depreciating Local Currency	
	Temporal	**Current Rate**	**Temporal**	**Current Rate**
*Liquidity Ratios**				
Current ratio (assuming subsidiary has inventory)	Lower	Higher	Higher	Lower
Quick ratio	Same	Same	Same	Same
A/R turnover	Same	Same	Same	Same
Inventory turnover	Uncertain	Uncertain	Uncertain	Uncertain
*Operating Efficiency Ratios**				
Fixed asset turnover	Higher	Lower	Lower	Higher
Total asset turnover	Higher	Lower	Lower	Higher
*Profitability Ratios**				
Gross profit margin	Higher	Lower	Lower	Higher
Net profit margin	Uncertain	Uncertain	Uncertain	Uncertain
ROE	Uncertain	Uncertain	Uncertain	Uncertain
ROA	Uncertain	Uncertain	Uncertain	Uncertain
*Financial Leverage Ratios**				
Interest coverage	Higher	Lower	Lower	Higher
LTD-to-total capital	Higher	Lower	Lower	Higher

* Ratios are calculated using end-of-period balance sheet numbers.

The Lessons We Learn

Cross-Reference to CFA Institute Assigned Topic Review #22

The material in this topic review provides a brief discussion of the lessons learned from recent accounting scandals and how transparency should help keep analysts from repeating past mistakes. Also, accounting for derivatives used for hedging purposes is introduced.

Common Earnings Measures

- *Earnings before interest, depreciation, and taxes* (EBITDA) is not an appropriate proxy for cash flow because is does not consider the changes in balance sheet operating accounts.
- *Operating earnings* are also referred to as *earnings before interest and taxes* (EBIT), operating income, and operating profit. It excludes the effects of financing and taxes.
- *Income from continuing operations* is earnings before extraordinary and nonrecurring items.
- *Net income* is the "bottom line" of the income statement. It includes all revenues, expenses, gains, losses, and "below the line" items.

Footnotes and Disclosures

It is necessary to examine the footnotes and other disclosures in order to evaluate whether nonoperating and nonrecurring transactions should be removed for analytical purposes.

Relationship Between Growth of Operating Cash Flow and Earnings

Over time, there should be a fairly stable relationship between the growth of operating cash flow and earnings. Earnings growth is not sustainable without the support of operating cash flow growth over the long-run.

Using Derivatives to Manage Risk

Figure 11: Summary of Hedge Types

	Purpose	*Recognition*
Fair value hedge	Offset exposure to changes in fair value of an asset or liability.	Gains and losses are recognized in the income statement.
Cash flow hedge	Offset exposure to variable cash flows from anticipated transactions.	Gains and losses are reported in equity. The gains and losses are eventually recognized in the income statement once the anticipated transaction affects earnings.
Net investment hedge of a foreign subsidiary	Offset exposure from an existing investment in a foreign subsidiary.	Gains and losses are recognized in equity along with translation gains and losses.

An effective hedge is one in which the change in fair value, cash flow, or net investment is exactly offset by changes in the hedging instrument. If the change in the hedging instrument is more or less than the change in value, cash flow, or net investment, the "extra" change is referred to as the portion of the hedge that is not effective.

Evaluating Financial Reporting Quality

Cross-Reference to CFA Institute Assigned Topic Review #23

Disaggregating accrual based income into a cash component and an accrual component enhances its predictive ability. Because the accrual component is less persistent than the cash component, an investor should apply a lower weighting to the accrual component.

Lower persistency is not always the result of strategic manipulation. Estimation errors can also be unintentional. However, if the investor fails to assign a lower weighting to the accrual component of the earnings, securities become mispriced.

Earnings quality usually refers to the persistence and sustainability of a firm's earnings. The following ratios can be used to measure earnings quality (higher ratio, lower earnings quality):

$$\text{balance sheet based accruals ratio} = \frac{(\text{NOA}_{\text{END}} - \text{NOA}_{\text{BEG}})}{(\text{NOA}_{\text{END}} + \text{NOA}_{\text{BEG}})/2}$$

$$\text{cash flow based accruals ratio} = \frac{(\text{NI} - \text{CFO} - \text{CFI})}{(\text{NOA}_{\text{END}} + \text{NOA}_{\text{BEG}})/2}$$

Earnings at extreme levels tend to revert back to normal levels over time (mean reversion); thus, extreme earnings (high or low) should not be expected to continue indefinitely. When earnings are largely comprised of accruals, mean reversion will occur even faster.

Manipulation techniques can be classified into the following categories:

- *Revenue recognition:* misstating revenue, accelerating revenue, and misclassifying nonrecurring or nonoperating revenue.
- *Expense recognition:* understating expenses, delaying expenses, and misclassifying ordinary expenses as nonrecurring or nonoperating.
- *Balance sheet manipulation:* off-balance sheet financing and goodwill.
- *Cash flow statement manipulation:* misclassifying cash flows, ignoring cash flows, and managing cash flows.

Different detection techniques exist for each category of manipulation techniques.

Revenue recognition:

- Look for large changes in receivables and unearned revenue.
- Look for increasing DSO.
- Compare revenue to actual cash collected.

Expense recognition:

- Look for large changes in fixed assets and inventory.
- Look for increasing DOH.
- Look for LIFO liquidation.
- Comparing depreciation expense (relative to gross plant and equipment) to other companies to determine the conservatism of the firm's estimates.
- Calculate core operating margin = (sales – COGS – SG&A) / sales.

Balance sheet:

- Capitalize operating leases.
- Look for lack of goodwill impairment.

Cash flow statement:

- Compare the growth of operating leases with the firm's asset growth.
- Be alert for a decrease in discretionary spending especially near year-end.

Integration of FSA Techniques

Cross-Reference to CFA Institute Assigned Topic Review #24

Financial Analysis Framework

The basic financial analysis framework involves:

1. Establishing objectives.
2. Collecting data.
3. Processing data.
4. Analyzing data.
5. Developing and communicating conclusions.
6. Following up.

Integration of FSA Techniques

1. Use the extended DuPont equation to examine the sources of earnings and performance.

2. Remove equity income from associates and the investment account to eliminate any bias.

3. Examine the composition of the balance sheet over time.

4. Determine if the capital structure can support future obligations and strategic plans by analyzing the components of long-term capital. Note that some liabilities don't necessarily result in an outflow of cash.

5. Segment disclosures are valuable in identifying the contribution to revenue and profit of each segment. Note the relationship between capital expenditures by segment and segment rates of return in order to evaluate capital spending decisions.

6. The balance sheet should be adjusted for off-balance-sheet financing activities. Capitalize operating leases for analytical purposes by increasing assets and liabilities by the present value of the remaining lease payments. Also, adjust the income statement by replacing rent expense with depreciation expense on the lease asset and interest expense on the lease liability.

7. Users must be aware of the proposed changes in accounting standards because of the financial statement effects and the potential impact on a firm's valuation. Earnings can be disaggregated into cash flow and accruals using either a balance sheet approach or a cash flow statement approach. For either measure, the lower the accruals ratio, the higher the earnings quality.

8. Earnings are considered higher quality when confirmed by cash flow. Cash flow can be compared to operating profit by adding back cash paid for interest and taxes to operating cash flow.

9. The standalone market value of a firm can be computed by eliminating the pro-rata market value of investments in associates. An implied P/E multiple can be computed by dividing the standalone market value by earnings not including equity income from associates.

CORPORATE FINANCE

Study Sessions 8 & 9

Topic Weight on Exam	5–15%
SchweserNotes™ Reference	Book 2, Pages 226–390

CAPITAL BUDGETING

Cross-Reference to CFA Institute Assigned Topic Review #25

Know the definitions of cash flow and the basic computations for expansion and replacement projects. For either type of project, we need to calculate the initial outlay (at $t = 0$), the annual incremental after-tax operating cash flows ($t = 1,\ldots,n$), and any additional terminal year cash flows ($t = n$).

Cash Flow Estimation for Expansion Projects

For an *expansion project*, the components of these cash flows are as follows:

Initial investment outlay. May include purchase price plus transportation and installation costs, additional costs such as training, and any required increase in net working capital.

After-tax operating cash flow (CF). Calculated as either of the following:

$$CF = (S - C - D)(1 - T) + D$$

$$= (S - C)(1 - T) + (TD)$$

where:
S = sales
C = cash operating costs
D = depreciation expense
T = marginal tax rate

Terminal year after-tax non-operating cash flow (TNOCF). Add the after-tax salvage value of the assets and any recapture of net working capital to the final year's after-tax operating cash flow.

$$TNOCF = Sal_T + NWCInv - T\,(Sal_T - B_T)$$

where:
Sal_T = cash proceeds from sale of fixed capital
B_T = book value of fixed capital

Cash Flow Estimation for Replacement Projects

For a *replacement project*, the process is similar, but:

- You must reduce the initial outlay by the after-tax proceeds of the sale of the existing asset.
- You must use only the *change* in depreciation that results from replacement.

If the new equipment has an expected life equal to the remaining life of the equipment to be replaced, then a positive NPV or IRR greater than the project cost of capital is sufficient to decide to replace the existing assets.

Be aware that the tax implications of the sale of assets can increase or decrease cash flow. If the sale price is greater than the carrying cost (book value) of the asset, tax must be paid on the gain; this decreases the after-tax sale proceeds. If the sale price is less than the book value, then taxes are reduced (and cash flow increased) by the tax rate times the amount of the loss.

Some points to remember in estimating incremental after-tax cash flows:

- Ignore sunk costs (any costs that are unaffected by the accept/reject decision).
- Ignore any financing costs associated with asset purchase (financing costs are included in the project cost of capital or WACC).
- Include any effects on the cash flows for other firm products (externalities).
- Include the opportunity cost (actual cash flows lost) of using any existing firm assets for the project.
- Shipping and installation costs are included in the initial cost used to calculate the annual depreciation for new assets.

Mutually Exclusive Projects With Unequal Lives

For *mutually exclusive projects with unequal lives*, the fact that the longer-lived project has a higher NPV is not sufficient to justify its acceptance.

There are two approaches to put the projects on an equal basis timewise:

The replacement chain approach. Assume that the shorter project will be repeated until the total number of years is equal to the years for the longer project. If we are comparing a 3-year and a 6-year project, we would project the cash flows as if we repeated the 3-year project at the end of year 3 and sum the cash flows to create a 6-year project for comparison.

We can then directly compare the NPV of the repeated project to the project with an expected life of six years and accept the one with the greater NPV (as long as the NPV is positive).

The equivalent annual annuity (EAA) *approach.* An alternative to the replacement chain approach is to convert the NPV for each project into an equivalent annual payment and select the project with the greater (positive) equivalent annual payment.

For a 3-year project with a net present value of NPV(3), the steps are as follows:

PV = NPV(3); FV = 0; N = 3; I/Y = WACC or project cost of capital; and compute PMT, which is the EAA of the 3-year project.

For a 6-year project with a net present value of NPV(6), the steps are as follows:

PV = NPV(6); FV = 0; N = 6; I/Y = WACC or project cost of capital; and compute PMT, which is the EAA of the 6-year project.

Project Risk Analysis

There are three techniques for estimating the stand-alone risk of a capital investment/project:

- *Sensitivity analysis.* Involves changing a variable such as sales volume, sales price, input cost, or the assumed cost of capital, and recalculating the NPV. The project with the greater percentage change in NPV for a given variable change is the riskier project.
- *Scenario analysis.* Calculate the NPV for "base-case," worst-case (low sales, low price, etc.), and a best-case scenario and assign probabilities to each of these outcomes. Then calculate the standard deviation of the NPV as you would with any probability model.

- *Monte Carlo simulation.* Use assumed probability distributions for the key variables in the NPV calculation, draw random values for these variables and calculate NPV (thousands of times), and use the distribution of NPVs to estimate the expected NPV and the standard deviation of NPV as a measure of stand-alone project risk.

Capital Rationing

Ideally, firms will continue to invest in positive return NPV projects until the marginal returns equal the marginal cost of capital. If a firm has insufficient capital to do this, it must ration its capital (allocate its funds) among the best possible combination of acceptable projects.

Capital rationing is the allocation of a fixed amount of capital among the set of available projects that will maximize shareholder wealth. A firm with less capital than profitable (i.e., positive NPV) projects should choose the combination of projects it can afford to fund that has the greatest total NPV. Remember, the goal with capital rationing is to maximize the overall NPV within the capital budget, not necessarily to select the individual projects with the highest NPV.

Using CAPM to Determine the Discount Rate

The CAPM can be used to determine the appropriate discount rate for a project based on risk. The project beta, $\beta_{project}$, is used as a measure of the systematic risk of the project, and the security market line (SML) estimates the project's required return as:

$$R_{project} = R_f + \beta_{project} [E(R_M) - R_f]$$

Real Options

Real options are similar to financial call and put options in that they give the option holder the right, but not the obligation, to make a decision. The difference is that real options are based on real assets rather than financial assets and are contingent on future events. Real options offer managers flexibility that can increase the NPV of individual projects.

Types of real options include the following:

- Timing options.
- Abandonment options.
- Expansion options.

- Flexibility options (price-setting and production-flexibility options).
- Fundamental options.

Approaches to Evaluating the Profitability of Real Options

- *Determine the NPV of the project without the option.* If the NPV of the project without the option is positive, the analyst knows that the project with the option must be even more valuable, and determining a specific value for the option is unnecessary.
- *Calculate the project NPV without the option and add the estimated value of the real option.*
- *Use decision trees.*
- *Use option pricing models.* Option pricing models are discussed in Study Session 17.

Accounting Income and Economic Income

Economic income is equal to the after-tax cash flow plus the change in the investment's market value. Interest is ignored and is instead included as a component of the discount rate.

economic income = after-tax cash flow – economic depreciation

where:
economic depreciation = (beginning market value – ending market value)

The economic income rate of return for each year (economic income/beginning market value) is equal to the project's required rate of return. This makes sense because the required return is the discount rate used to determine the value of the investment.

Accounting income is the reported net income on a company's financial statements that results from an investment in a project.

There are two key factors that account for the *differences between economic and accounting income:*

1. Accounting depreciation is based on the original cost of the investment, while economic depreciation is based on the change in market value of the investment.

2. The after-tax cost of debt (interest expense) is subtracted from net income, while financing costs for determining economic income are reflected in the discount rate.

Other Valuation Models

Alternative forms of determining income should theoretically lead to the same calculated NPV if applied correctly.

- *Economic profit* is calculated as NOPAT – $WACC. Economic profit reflects the income earned by all capital holders and is therefore discounted at the WACC to determine the market value added (MVA), or NPV, of the investment.
- *Residual income* is focused on returns to equity holders and is calculated as net income less an equity charge. Residual income reflects the income to equity holders only and is discounted at the required return on equity to determine NPV.
- *Claims valuation* separates cash flows based on the claims that equity holders and debt holders have on the asset. Cash flows to debt holders are discounted at the cost of debt, and cash flows to equity holders are discounted at the cost of equity. The present value of each set of cash flows is added together to determine the value of the firm.

Economic profit models and residual income models are discussed in more detail in Study Session 12.

Capital Structure and Leverage

Cross-Reference to CFA Institute Assigned Topic Review #26

Objective of the Capital Structure Decision

The objective of a company's *capital structure decision* is to determine the optimal proportion of debt and equity financing that will minimize the firm's weighted average cost of capital (WACC). This is also the capital structure that will maximize the value of the firm.

Capital Structure Theory

MM Proposition I (No Taxes)—capital structure is irrelevant; value of the firm is unaffected by the capital structure. $V_L = V_U$

MM Proposition II (No Taxes)—the cost of equity increases linearly as a company increases its proportion of debt financing. The benefits from using more debt are exactly offset by the rise in the cost of equity, resulting in no change in the firm's WACC.

Figure 1: MM Proposition II (No Taxes)

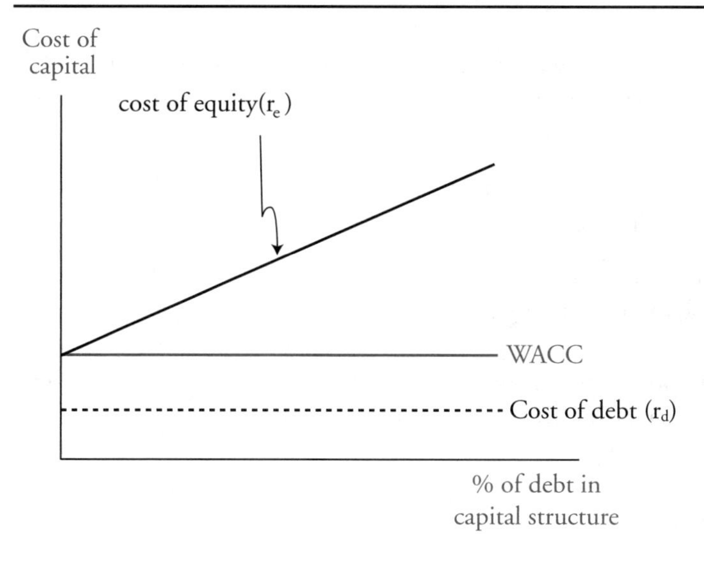

MM Proposition I (With Taxes)—Value is maximized at 100% debt; the tax shield provided by debt causes the WACC to decline as leverage increases.
$V_L = V_U + (t \times d)$

MM Proposition II (With Taxes)—WACC is minimized at 100% debt; the tax shield provided by debt causes the WACC to decline as leverage increases.

Figure 2: MM Proposition II (With Taxes)

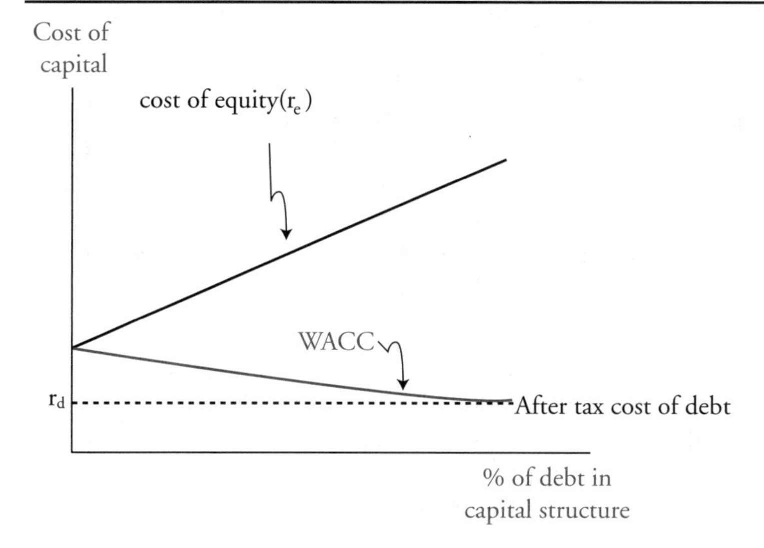

Costs and Their Potential Effect on the Capital Structure

Costs of financial distress are the increased costs companies face when earnings decline and the company has trouble paying its interest costs. The expected costs of financial distress for a firm have two components:

1. Direct and indirect costs of financial distress and bankruptcy.
2. Probability of financial distress.

In general, higher amounts of leverage result in greater expected costs of financial distress and a higher probability of financial distress.

The **net agency costs** of equity are the costs associated with the conflict of interest between a company's managers and owners, and consist of three components:

1. Monitoring costs.
2. Bonding costs.
3. Residual losses.

Costs of *asymmetric information* result from managers having more information about a firm than investors.

The Capital Structure Decision

With regard to management's decisions regarding capital structure:

- *MM's propositions with no taxes* says that capital structure is irrelevant.
- *MM's propositions with taxes* says that the tax shield provided by interest expense makes borrowing valuable, and the value of the firm is maximized, and the WACC is minimized, at 100% debt.
- *Pecking order theory* states that managers prefer financing choices that send the least visible signal to investors, with internal capital being most preferred, debt being next, and raising equity externally the least preferred method of financing.
- *Static trade-off theory* states that managers will try to balance the benefits of debt with the costs of financial distress. The static trade-off theory seeks to balance the costs of financial distress with the tax shield benefits from using debt, and states there is an optimal capital structure that has an optimal proportion of debt.

If we remove the assumption that there are no costs of financial distress, there comes a point where the additional value added by the tax shield from borrowing another dollar is exceeded by the value-reducing expected costs of financial distress from the additional borrowing. This point represents the optimal capital structure for a firm where the WACC is minimized as the value of the firm is maximized.

Accounting for the costs of financial distress, the expression for the value of a levered firm becomes:

$$V_L = V_U + (t \times d) - PV(\text{costs of financial distress})$$

Note that the previous equation and Figure 3 represent the static trade-off theory just discussed.

Figure 3: Static Trade-Off Theory: Firm Value vs. Capital Structure

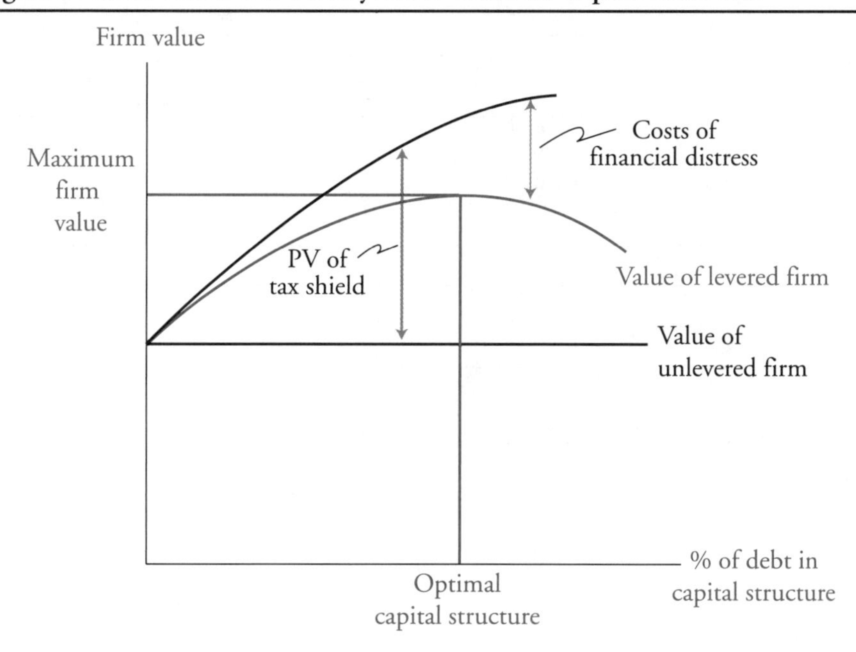

Factors to Consider for Analysis

Factors an analyst should consider when evaluating a firm's capital structure include:

- Changes in the firm's capital structure over time.
- Capital structure of competitors with similar business risk.
- Factors affecting agency costs such as the quality of corporate governance.

International Differences

Major factors that influence *international differences* in financial leverage include:

- Institutional, legal, and taxation factors.
- Financial market and banking system factors.
- Macroeconomic factors.

Figure 4: Impact of Country-Specific Factors on Capital Structure

Country Specific Factor	*Use of Total Debt*	*Maturity of Debt*
Institutional and Legal Factors		
Strong legal system	Lower	Longer
Less information asymmetry	Lower	Longer
Favorable tax rates on dividends	Lower	N/A
Financial Market Factors		
More liquid stock and bond markets	N/A	Longer
Greater reliance on banking system	Higher	N/A
Greater institutional investor presence	Lower	Longer
Macroeconomic Factors		
Higher inflation	Lower	Shorter
Higher GDP growth	N/A	Longer

Dividends and Dividend Policy

Cross-Reference to CFA Institute Assigned Topic Review #27

Dividend Theories

Merton Miller and Franco Modigliani (MM) maintain that *dividend policy* is irrelevant, as it has no effect on the price of a firm's stock or its cost of capital. MM's argument of dividend irrelevance is based on their concept of *homemade dividends*. Dividend preference theory says investors prefer the certainty of current cash to future capital gains. Tax aversion theory states that investors are tax averse to dividends and would prefer companies instead buy back shares, especially when the tax rate on dividends is higher than the tax rate on capital gains.

Signaling Effect

The signaling effect of dividend changes is based on the idea that dividends convey information about future earnings from management to investors (who have less information about a firm's prospects than management). In general, unexpected increases are good news and unexpected decreases are bad news as seen by U.S. investors.

Clientele Effect

Clientele effect refers to the varying preferences for dividends of different groups of investors, such as individuals, institutions, and corporations. Companies structure their dividend policies consistent with preferences of their clienteles. Miller and Modigliani, however, note that once all the clienteles are satisfied, changing the dividend policy would only entail changing clienteles and would not affect firm value.

Taxation

A **double-taxation system** is used in the United States to tax dividends paid. Earnings are taxed at the corporate level regardless of whether they are distributed as dividends, and dividends are taxed again at the shareholder level.

$$\text{effective rate} = \text{corporate tax rate} + (1 - \text{corporate tax rate}) \times (\text{individual tax rate})$$

A **split-rate** corporate tax system taxes earnings distributed as dividends at a lower rate than earnings that are retained. The effect is to offset the higher (double) tax rate applied to dividends at the individual level.

Under an **imputation tax system**, taxes are paid at the corporate level but are attributed to the shareholder, so that *all taxes are effectively paid at the shareholder rate.*

Stable Dividend Policy

A firm with a stable dividend policy could use a target payout adjustment model to gradually move towards its target payout.

$$\text{expected dividend} = \begin{pmatrix}\text{previous}\\\text{dividend}\end{pmatrix} + \left[\begin{pmatrix}\text{expected}\\\text{increase}\\\text{in EPS}\end{pmatrix} \times \begin{pmatrix}\text{target}\\\text{payout}\\\text{ratio}\end{pmatrix} \times \begin{pmatrix}\text{adjustment}\\\text{factor}\end{pmatrix}\right]$$

where:
adjustment factor = 1 / number of years over which the adjustment in dividends will take place

Share Repurchases

There are five common rationales for share repurchases (versus dividends):

1. Potential tax advantages: When capital gains are taxed favorably as compared to dividends.
2. Share price support/signaling: Management wants to signal better prospects for the firm.
3. Added flexibility: Reduces the need for "sticky" dividends in the future.
4. Offsets dilution from employee stock options.
5. Increases financial leverage by reducing equity in the balance sheet.

Dividend Coverage Ratios

The two most important predictors of dividend reliability are:

dividend coverage ratio = net income / dividends

FCFE coverage ratio = FCFE / (dividends + share repurchases)

Corporate Governance

Cross-Reference to CFA Institute Assigned Topic Review #28

Corporate governance is defined by McEnally and Kim as the "system of principles, policies, procedures, and clearly defined responsibilities and accountabilities used by stakeholders to overcome conflicts of interest inherent in the corporate form." Note that conflicts of interest are most severe in corporations because of the separation of ownership and management (versus sole proprietorship or partnership), so the focus is on corporate governance in primarily corporations.

An *agency relationship* occurs when an individual, who is referred to as the "agent," acts on behalf of another individual, who is referred to as the "principal." Such a relationship creates the potential for a principal-agent problem where the agent may act for his own well-being rather than that of the principal. Corporate governance systems are primarily concerned with potential principal-agent problems in two areas: (1) between managers and shareholders, and (2) between directors and shareholders.

Examples of ways that management may act for its own interests rather than those of shareholders include the following:

- Expanding the size of the firm for the benefit of management, not shareholder value.
- Granting excessive compensation and perquisites.
- Investing in ventures with returns too small to justify the risk.
- Not taking enough risk.

The following are guidelines for corporate governance best practices to remember for the exam:

- 75% of board members are independent.
- CEO and chairman are separate positions.
- Directors are knowledgeable and experienced and serve on only two or three boards.
- The board holds annual elections (not staggered elections).
- The board is annually evaluated and assessed.
- Board members meet annually without management present.
- The finance committee includes only independent directors with finance expertise, and the committee meets annually with auditors.
- Only independent directors serve on the nominating committee.
- Most of senior management's compensation is tied to performance.
- The board uses independent and outside counsel.
- The board is required to approve any related-party transactions.

The key is to remember the link between valuation and corporate governance. Empirical studies show that:

- Strong corporate governance increases profitability and shareholder returns.
- Weak corporate governance decreases company value by increasing risk to shareholders.

Mergers and Acquisitions

Cross-Reference to CFA Institute Assigned Topic Review #29

Categorization

- *Statutory merger*. The target ceases to exist and all assets and liabilities become part of the acquirer.
- *Subsidiary merger*. The target company becomes a subsidiary of the acquirer.
- *Consolidations*. Both companies cease to exist in their prior form and come together to form a new company.

Types

- *Horizontal mergers.* Firms in similar lines of business combine.
- *Vertical mergers.* Combine firms either further up or down the supply chain.
- *Conglomerate mergers.* Combine firms in unrelated businesses.

Motivations

Common motivations behind M&A activity include the following:

- Achieving synergies.
- Growing more rapidly.
- Increasing market power.
- Gaining access to unique capabilities.
- Diversifying.
- Gaining personal benefits for managers.
- Taking advantage of tax benefits.
- Unlocking hidden value for a struggling company.
- Achieving international business goals.
- Bootstrapping earnings.

Bootstrapping is a technique whereby a high P/E firm acquires a low P/E firm in an exchange of stock. The total earnings of the combined firm are unchanged, but the total shares outstanding are less than the two separate entities. The result is higher reported earnings per share, even though there may be no economic gains.

Motivations and Industry Life Cycles

Figure 5: Merger Motivations in the Industry Life Cycle

Industry Life Cycle Stage	*Industry Characteristics*	*Merger Motivation*	*Common Types of Mergers*
Pioneer/ development	• Unsure of product acceptance • Large capital requirements and low profit margins	• Gain access to capital from more mature businesses • Share management talent	• Conglomerate • Horizontal
Rapid growth	• High profit margins • Accelerating sales and earnings • Competition still low	• Gain access to capital • Expand capacity to grow	• Conglomerate • Horizontal
Mature growth	• Lots of new competition • Still opportunities for above average growth	• Increase operational efficiencies • Economies of scale/synergies	• Horizontal • Vertical
Stabilization	• Competition has reduced growth potential • Capacity constraints	• Economies of scale/reduce costs • Improve management	• Horizontal
Decline	• Consumer tastes have shifted • Overcapacity/ shrinking profit margins	• Survival • Operational efficiencies • Acquire new growth opportunities	• Horizontal • Vertical • Conglomerate

Transaction Characteristics

- *Stock purchase*. The target's shareholders receive cash or shares of the acquiring company's stock in exchange for their shares of the target.
- *Asset purchase*. The payment is made directly to the target company in return for specific assets.

Figure 6: Key Differences Between Forms of Acquisition

	Stock Purchase	*Asset Purchase*
Payment	Made directly to target company shareholders in exchange for their shares	Made directly to target company
Approval	Majority shareholder approval required	No shareholder approval needed unless asset sale is substantial
Corporate taxes	None	Target company pays capital gains taxes
Shareholder taxes	Shareholders pay capital gains tax	None
Liabilities	Acquirer assumes liabilities of target	Acquirer usually avoids assumption of target's liabilities

Method of Payment

The method of payment in a merger transaction may be cash, stock, or a combination of the two. Cash offerings are straight forward, but in a stock offering, the exchange ratio determines the number of the acquirer's shares that each target company shareholder will receive.

When an acquirer is negotiating with a target over the method of payment, there are three main factors that should be considered:

1. Distribution between risk and reward for the acquirer and target shareholders.
2. Relative valuations of companies involved.
3. Changes in capital structure.

Attitude of Target Management

In a friendly merger, the acquirer and target work together to perform due diligence and sign a definitive merger agreement before submitting the merger proposal to the target's shareholders.

In a hostile merger, the acquirer seeks to avoid the target's management through a tender offer or proxy battle. If the target company's management does not support the deal, the acquirer submits a merger proposal directly to the target's board of directors in a process called a *bear hug*. If the bear hug is unsuccessful, the next step is to appeal directly to the target's shareholders using one of two methods—a tender offer or a proxy battle.

1. In a *tender offer*, the acquirer offers to buy the shares directly from the target shareholders, and each individual shareholder either accepts or rejects the offer.

2. In a *proxy battle*, the acquirer seeks to control the target by having shareholders approve a new "acquirer approved" board of directors. A proxy solicitation is approved by regulators and then sent to the target's shareholders.

Takeover Defense Mechanisms

Pre-offer defense mechanisms:

- Poison pills.
- Poison puts.
- Reincorporating in a state with restrictive takeover laws.
- Staggered board elections.
- Restricted voting rights.
- Supermajority voting.
- Fair price amendments.
- Golden parachutes.

Post-offer defense mechanisms:

- "Just say no" defense.
- Litigation, greenmail.
- Share repurchases.
- Leveraged recapitalizations.
- "Crown jewel" defense.
- "Pac man" defense.
- Finding a white knight or white squire.

Herfindahl-Hirschman Index (HHI)

$$\text{HHI} = \sum_{i=1}^{n} (\text{MS}_i \times 100)^2$$

Figure 7: HHI Concentration Level and Likelihood of Antitrust Action

Post-Merger HHI	*Industry Concentration*	*Change in Pre- and Post-Merger HHI*	*Antitrust Action*
Less than 1,000	Not concentrated	Any amount	No action
Between 1,000 and 1,800	Moderately concentrated	100 or more	Possible antitrust challenge
Greater than 1,800	Highly concentrated	50 or more	Antitrust challenge virtually certain

Valuing a Merger Target

Discounted Cash Flow

To calculate free cash flow (FCF) for a target company and estimate its value using DCF analysis, we can use the following steps:

Step 1: Determine which free cash flow model to use for the analysis.
Step 2: Develop pro forma financial estimates.
Step 3: Calculate free cash flows using the pro forma data.
Step 4: Discount free cash flows back to the present at the appropriate discount rate.
Step 5: Determine the terminal value and discount it back to the present.
Step 6: Add the discounted FCF values for the first stage and the terminal value to determine the value of the target firm.

Advantages:

- It is relatively easy to model any changes in the target company's cash flow that may occur after the merger.
- It is based on forecasts of fundamental conditions in the future rather than on current data.
- It is easy to customize.

Disadvantages:

- The model is difficult to apply when free cash flows are negative.
- Estimates of cash flows and earnings are highly subject to error, especially when those estimates are for time periods far in the future.
- Discount rate changes over time can have a large impact on the valuation estimate.
- Estimation error is a major concern since the majority of the estimated value for the target is based on the terminal value, which is highly sensitive to estimates used for the constant growth rate and discount rate.

Comparable Company Analysis

Comparable company analysis uses relative valuation metrics for similar firms to determine a market value for the target, and then adds a takeover premium to this value.

Step 1: Identify the set of comparable firms.
Step 2: Calculate various relative value measures based on the current market prices of companies in the sample.
Step 3: Calculate descriptive statistics for the relative value metrics and apply those measures to the target firm.
Step 4: Estimate a takeover premium.
Step 5: Calculate the estimated takeover price for the target as the sum of estimated stock value based on comparables and the takeover premium.

Advantages:

- Data for comparable companies is easy to access.
- Assumption that similar assets should have similar values is fundamentally sound.
- Estimates of value are derived directly from the market rather than assumptions and estimates about the future.

Disadvantages:

- The approach implicitly assumes that the market's valuation of the comparable companies is accurate.
- Using comparable companies provides an estimate of a fair stock price, but not a fair takeover price. An appropriate takeover premium must be determined separately.
- It is difficult to incorporate merger synergies or changing capital structures into the analysis.
- Historical data used to estimate a takeover premium may not be timely, and therefore may not reflect current conditions in the M&A market.

Comparable Transaction Analysis

Comparable transaction analysis uses relative valuation metrics from recent takeover transactions so there is no need to calculate a separate takeover premium.

Step 1: Identify a set of recent takeover transactions.
Step 2: Calculate various relative value measures based on completed deal prices for the companies in the sample.
Step 3: Calculate descriptive statistics for the relative value metrics and apply those measures to the target firm.

Advantages:

- Since the approach uses data from actual transactions, there is no need to estimate a separate takeover premium.
- Estimates of value are derived directly from recent prices for actual deals completed in the marketplace rather than from assumptions and estimates about the future.
- Use of prices established by recent transactions reduces the risk that the target's shareholders could file a lawsuit against the target's managers and board of directors for mispricing the deal.

Disadvantages:

- The approach implicitly assumes that the M&A market valued past transactions accurately. If past transactions were over or underpriced, the mispricings will be carried over to the estimated value for the target.
- There may not be enough comparable transactions to develop a reliable data set for use in calculating the estimated target value. If the analyst isn't able to find enough similar companies, she may try to use M&A deals from other industries that are not similar enough to the deal being considered.
- It is difficult to incorporate merger synergies or changing capital structures into the analysis.

Evaluating a Merger Bid

Post-merger valuation for an acquirer: $V_{AT} = V_A + V_T + S - C$

Professor's Note: The pre-merger value of the target should be the price of the target stock before any market speculation causes the target's stock prices to jump.

Gains accrued to the target: $\text{gain}_T = TP = P_T - V_T$

Gains accrued to the acquirer: $\text{gain}_A = S - TP = S - (P_T - V_T)$

With a cash offer, the target firm's shareholders will profit by the amount paid over its current share price (i.e., the takeover premium). However, this gain is capped at that amount. *With a stock offer*, the gains will be determined in part by the value of the combined firm, because the target firm's shareholders do not receive cash and just walk away, but rather retain ownership in the new firm. Accordingly, for a stock deal we must adjust our formula for the price of the target: $P_T = (N \times P_{AT})$.

Effect of Price and Payment Method

The *acquirer will want to pay the lowest* possible price (the premerger value of the target, V_T), while the *target wants to receive the highest* possible price (the premerger value of the target plus the expected synergies, $V_T + S$).

In a *cash offer*, the acquirer assumes the risk and receives the potential reward from the merger, while the gain for the target shareholders is limited to the takeover premium. If an acquirer makes a cash offer in a deal, but the synergies realized are greater than expected, the takeover premium for the target would remain unchanged while the acquirer reaps the additional reward. Likewise, if synergies were less than expected, the target would still receive the same takeover premium, but the acquirer's gain may evaporate.

In a *stock offer*, some of the risks and potential rewards from the merger shift to the target firm. When the target receives stock as payment, the target's shareholders become a part owner of the acquiring company. This means that if estimates of the potential synergies are wrong, the target will share in the upside if the actual synergies exceed expectations, but will also share in the downside if the actual synergies are below expectations.

The more confident both parties are that synergies will be realized, the more the acquirer will prefer to pay cash and the more the target will prefer to receive stock.

Types of Restructuring

- *Cash divestitures* involve a direct sale of a division to an outside party in exchange for cash.
- *Equity carve-outs* create a new independent company by giving a proportionate equity interest in a subsidiary to outside shareholders through a public offering of stock.
- *Spin-offs* create a new independent company by distributing shares to existing shareholders of the parent company.
- *Split-offs* allow shareholders to receive new shares of a division of the parent company by exchanging a portion of their parent company shares.
- *Liquidations* break up the firm and sell its assets piece by piece. Most liquidations are associated with bankruptcy.

Voluntary Divestitures

The reasons why a company may divest assets include the following:

- A division no longer fitting into management's strategy.
- Poor profitability for a division.
- Reverse synergy.
- To receive an infusion of cash.

EQUITY

Study Sessions 10, 11, & 12

Topic Weight on Exam	20–30%
SchweserNotes™ Reference	Book 3, Pages 9–270

EQUITY VALUATION: APPLICATIONS AND PROCESS

Cross-Reference to CFA Institute Assigned Topic Review #30

Intrinsic value is the estimate of an asset's value that would be made by someone who has complete understanding of the characteristics of the asset and its issuing firm. To the extent that market prices are not perfectly (informationally) efficient, they may diverge from intrinsic values. The difference between an analyst's estimate of a security's intrinsic value and its market price has two components—the difference between the security's *actual* intrinsic value and its market price, and the difference between the security's actual intrinsic value and the analyst's estimate of the intrinsic value:

$$IV_{analyst} - price = (IV_{actual} - price) + (IV_{analyst} - IV_{actual})$$

The **going concern assumption** is simply the assumption that a company will continue to operate as a business (as opposed to going out of business). **Liquidation value** is an estimate of what the assets of the firm would bring if sold separately, net of the company's liabilities.

Equity valuation is the process of estimating the value of an asset by (1) using a model based on the variables the analyst believes determine the fundamental value of the asset or (2) comparing it to the observable market value of "similar" assets. Equity valuation models are used by analysts in a number of ways including stock selection, forecasting the value impact of corporate actions, providing fairness opinions, communication with analysts and investors, valuation of private firms, portfolio management, and asset allocation.

The **five elements of industry structure** that determine the competitive environment in which firms compete and drive successful competitive strategy (as developed by Professor Michael Porter) are:

1. Threat of new entrants in the industry.
2. Threat of substitutes.
3. Bargaining power of buyers.
4. Bargaining power of suppliers.
5. Rivalry among existing competitors.

The basic building blocks of equity valuation come from accounting information contained in the firm's reports and releases.

Quality of earnings issues can be broken down into several categories and may be addressed only in the footnotes and disclosures to the financial statements:

1. Accelerating or premature recognition of income.
2. Reclassifying gains and non-operating income.
3. Expense recognition and losses.
4. Amortization, depreciation, and discount rates.
5. Off-balance-sheet issues.

An **absolute valuation model** refers to one which estimates intrinsic value based on future earnings, cash flows, and risk. Dividend discount and free cash flow valuation models are examples of absolute valuation models.

A **relative valuation model** estimates the value of a security relative to market prices of other similar securities. Valuation based on price-to-earnings, price-to-cash flow, and price-to sales ratios of other securities or securities indexes are examples of relative valuation models.

In **choosing a valuation model**, the analyst should consider the purpose of the analysis and the characteristics of the firm, including whether it pays dividends, the stability of its cash flows, how well its earnings growth can be estimated, and the nature of its assets.

Return Concepts

Cross-Reference to CFA Institute Assigned Topic Review #31

Holding period return is the increase in price of an asset plus any cash flow received from that asset, divided by the initial price of the asset. The holding period can be any length. Usually, it is assumed the cash flow comes at the end of the period:

$$\text{holding period return} = r = \frac{P_1 - P_0 + CF_1}{P_0} = \frac{P_1 + CF_1}{P_0} - 1$$

An asset's required return is the minimum expected return an investor requires given the asset's characteristics.

If expected return is greater (less) than required return, the asset is undervalued (overvalued). The mispricing can lead to a return from convergence of price to intrinsic value.

The equity risk premium (called the market risk premium in the CAPM context) is the return over the risk-free rate that investors require for holding equity securities.

equity risk premium = required return on equity index – risk-free rate

A historical estimate of the equity risk premium consists of the difference between the mean return on a broad-based, equity-market index and the mean return on U.S. Treasury bills over a given time period.

There are four types of estimates of the equity risk premium: (1) historical estimates, (2) forward-looking estimates, (3) macroeconomic model estimates, and (4) survey estimates.

1. The historical estimates are straightforward to compute, but they are not current.
2. Forward-looking estimates use current information, but that information needs to be updated periodically as new estimates are generated.
3. Macroeconomic models use current information, but they are only appropriate for developed countries where public equities represent a relatively large share of the economy.
4. Survey estimates are easy to obtain, but there can be a wide disparity between opinions.

Models used to estimate the equity risk premium:

- Gordon growth model:

$$(D_1 / P) + \hat{g} - r_{LT,0}$$

- Ibbotsen-Chen (supply side)

$$\text{equity risk premium} = [1+\hat{i}]\times[1+\widehat{rEg}]\times[1+\widehat{PEg}]-1+\hat{Y}-\widehat{RF}$$

Models used to estimate the required return on equity:

- CAPM:

$$\text{required return on stock j} = \text{risk-free return} + (\text{equity risk premium}) \times (\text{beta of j})$$

- Multifactor model:

$$\text{required return} = RF + (\text{risk premium})_1 + \ldots + (\text{risk premium})_n$$

- Fama-French model:

$$\text{req. ret. of stock j} = RF + \beta_{mkt,j} \times (R_{mkt} - RF) + \beta_{SMB,j} \times (R_{small} - R_{big}) + \beta_{HML,j} \times (R_{HBM} - R_{LBM})$$

where:
$(R_{mkt} - RF)$ = market risk premium
$(R_{small} - R_{big})$ = small-cap risk premium
$(R_{HBM} - R_{LBM})$ = value risk premium

- The Pastor-Stambaugh model adds a liquidity factor to the Fama-French model.
- Macroeconomic multifactor models use factors associated with economic variables that would affect the cash flows and/or discount rate of companies.
- The build-up method is similar to the risk premium approach. One difference is that this approach does not use betas to adjust for the exposure to a factor. The bond yield plus risk premium method is a type of build-up method.

Beta estimation:

- A regression of the returns of a publicly-traded company's stock returns on the returns of an index provides an estimate of beta. For forecasting required returns using the CAPM, an analyst may wish to adjust for beta drift using the Blume method:

$$\text{adjusted beta} = (2/3) \times (\text{regression beta}) + (1/3) \times (1.0)$$

- For thinly-traded stocks and non-publicly traded companies, an analyst can estimate beta using a four-step process: (1) identify publicly traded benchmark company; (2) estimate the beta of the benchmark company; (3) unlever the benchmark company's beta; and (4) relever the beta using the capital structure of the thinly-traded/non-public company.

Each of the various methods of estimating the required return on an equity investment has strengths and weaknesses.

- The CAPM is simple but may have low explanatory power.
- Multifactor models have more explanatory power but are more complex and costly.
- Build-up models are simple and can apply to closely held companies, but they typically use historical values as estimates that may or may not be relevant to the current situation.

The Five Competitive Forces that Shape Strategy

Cross-Reference to CFA Institute Assigned Topic Review #32

This is important material which has been in the curriculum for many years. Analysis of a firm requires an understanding of the firm's competitive environment. Two central questions provide the basis for the firm's choice of a competitive strategy:

1. *Industry attractiveness.* Is the industry attractive in terms of long-term profitability potential?

2. *Competitive advantage.* What determines a firm's relative competitive position within an industry?

Porter's Five Forces

Five forces determine the industry's degree of competitiveness and long-term profit potential. Memorize them!

1. *Entry barriers* (or threat of new entrants) for new competitors are a function of economies of scale, product differentials, brand identity, capital requirements, access to distribution channels, government policy, and cost advantages.

2. The *threat of substitutes* is a function of relative price performance of substitutes, buyer propensity to substitute, and switching cost.

3. *Bargaining power of buyers* is a function of bargaining leverage and price sensitivity.

4. *Bargaining power of suppliers* is determined by differentiation of inputs, presence of substitute inputs, supplier concentration, importance of volume to the supplier, and threat of forward integration.

5. *Rivalry among existing competitors* is a function of industry growth, fixed costs, value added, product differences, brand identity, diversity of competitors, exit barriers, and informational complexity.

You should be able to read a short description of an industry and then discuss how each of these factors contributes to the long-term attractiveness (or profitability) of the industry. *Memorize the five forces!*

DCF Methods

Discounted cash flow (DCF) valuation is based on the idea that the value today of any security is the discounted value of all future cash flows.

Dividend discount models (DDMs). The DDM defines cash flow as dividends to be received in the future. This is based on the idea that, over time, earnings and dividends will converge. The DDM is most appropriate for mature and profitable firms that are not engaged in a fast-growing segment of the economy, or for large, diversified portfolios like the S&P 500. Use the DDM for valuation problems with the following characteristics:

- The firm has a dividend history.
- The dividend policy is consistent and related to earnings.
- The perspective is that of a minority shareholder.

Free cash flow (FCF) *models*. Cash flow from a security can also be defined as free cash flow. Two versions of FCF valuation exist: FCF to the firm (FCFF) and FCF to equity (FCFE). FCFF is the cash flow generated by the firm above that required to be reinvested to maintain current operations. FCFE is FCFF minus debt service and preferred dividends. FCF valuation is appropriate when the following characteristics exist:

- The firm does not have a stable dividend policy.
- The firm has a dividend policy that is not related to earnings.
- The firm's FCF is related to profitability.
- The perspective is that of a controlling shareholder.

Residual income (RI). Residual income refers to the amount of earnings during the period that exceed the investor's required earnings. Think of residual income as *economic profit*. In this framework, the value of the firm's equity is the firm's book value plus the present value of all future residual income. The RI method can be difficult to apply because it requires an in-depth analysis of the firm's accounting accruals.

The RI method is most appropriate under the following conditions:

- The firm does not have a dividend history.
- The firm's FCF is negative.
- It is a firm with transparent and high quality accounting.

In all cases, you will have to forecast the future cash flows (dividends, free cash flow, or residual income), determine the appropriate discount rate, and discount the cash flows to obtain the value of the firm. For the DDM, FCFE, and RI methods, the appropriate discount rate is the cost of equity. In general, there are three methods for determining the cost of equity:

1. The CAPM:

$$E(r) = r_f + \{\beta \times [E(r_m) - r_f]\}$$

2. Multifactor models such as the Arbitrage Pricing Theory or the Fama French Model.

3. The build-up method, such as adding a risk premium to the firm's bond yield.

For the FCFF model, the appropriate discount rate is the weighted average cost of capital (WACC).

Now let's turn to the specifics of the valuation methods.

Discounted Dividend Valuation

Cross-Reference to CFA Institute Assigned Topic Review #33

There are four versions of the multiperiod DDM: (1) the Gordon growth model, (2) 2-stage growth model, (3) H-model, and (4) 3-stage growth model. We will review only the first three, since the 3-stage model is an extension of the 2-stage version.

Gordon Growth Model

The *Gordon growth model* assumes that dividends will grow at a constant rate forever. The formula is as follows:

$$V_0 = \frac{D_0(1+g)}{r-g} = \frac{D_1}{r-g}$$

The constant growth rate in dividends and earnings is g. Note that the value today, V_0, is dependent on the amount of the dividend one period from today, D_1. The model also assumes that r is greater than g. You can solve the Gordon model for either r or g to determine the required return or growth rate implicit in the current market price.

Professor's Note: If you're using the Gordon model on the exam, make sure you have next year's dividend, D_1. If you are given the current dividend, D_0, you can get next year's dividend as: $D_1 = D_0 \times (1 + g)$.

A related construct is the *present value of growth opportunities* (PVGO). This simply says that the value of the stock today is equal to its nongrowth value (E / r) plus the PVGO:

$$V_0 = \frac{E}{r} + PVGO$$

The main use of this idea is to plug in the current market price as V_0 and calculate the PVGO implied in the market price (large PVGO indicates high expected growth).

The Gordon growth model is most appropriate for mature, stable firms. The limitations of the Gordon model include the following:

- Valuations are very sensitive to estimates of r and g.
- The model assumes that the firm is paying dividends now, or will be during the foreseeable future.
- Unpredictable growth patterns from some firms make using the model difficult.

Two-Stage Growth Model

The multistage models are somewhat more complex. Basically, the multistage models (e.g., the 2-stage growth model and the H-model) *assume that there is some temporary short-term growth period followed by a stable long-term growth period.* The 2-stage model normally assumes that the firm will experience a high rate of growth for the next few years followed by low growth for eternity.

The value of the stock is the present value of the dividends during the high-growth period plus the present value of the terminal value. The terminal value can be estimated using the Gordon growth model or a market multiple approach.

H-Model

The H-model assumes that growth is currently high, but decreases at a linear rate toward the low-growth rate. Once the low-growth rate is reached, the H-model assumes that the low-growth rate will prevail forever. The difference between the two models is how the growth rate changes from high growth to low growth. The 2-stage model assumes that the change happens at one point in time. The H-model assumes that the growth rate declines in a linear fashion from the current (high) growth rate to the long-term (stable) growth rate over *t* years.

The approximate value of a firm's equity using the H-model is:

$$V_0 = \frac{D_0 \times (1+g_L)}{r-g_L} + \frac{D_0 \times H \times (g_S - g_L)}{r-g_L}$$

where:

$H = \left(\frac{t}{2}\right)$ = half-life (in years) of high-growth period
t = length of high-growth period
g_S = short-term growth rate
g_L = long-term growth rate
r = required return

Note that the second term is the value of growth in excess of g_L and that the first is the value of the firm with constant growth of g_L.

Solving for Required Return

You can use any of the models to solve for the required rate of return given the other model inputs. For the multistage models, the algebra gets complex and is very unlikely to show up on the exam.

For the Gordon (or stable growth) model, solving for return yields:

$$r = \frac{D_1}{P_0} + g$$

This is a handy tool for backing into the required rate of return.

The Sustainable Growth Rate

The *sustainable growth rate* (SGR) is defined as the rate that earnings (and dividends) can continue to grow indefinitely, given that a firm's capital structure is unchanged and it doesn't issue any new equity. SGR can be derived from the relationship between the firm's retention rate and ROE as determined by the DuPont formula:

$$g = \left(\frac{\text{net income} - \text{dividends}}{\text{net income}}\right) \times \left(\frac{\text{net income}}{\text{sales}}\right) \times \left(\frac{\text{sales}}{\text{total assets}}\right) \times \left(\frac{\text{total assets}}{\text{stockholders' equity}}\right)$$

This has also been called the *PRAT model*, where SGR is a function of the profit margin (P), the retention rate (R), the asset turnover (A), and the degree of financial leverage (T). Unless otherwise instructed on the exam, use beginning-of-period balance sheet value to calculate SGR and to construct the DuPont model.

Free Cash Flow Valuation

Cross-Reference to CFA Institute Assigned Topic Review #34

Free cash flow to the firm (FCFF) is the cash available to all of the firm's investors, including common stockholders, preferred stockholders, and bondholders after the firm buys and sells products, provides services, pays its cash operating expenses, and makes short- and long-term investments. *Free cash flow to equity* (FCFE) is the cash available to the common stockholders after funding capital requirements, working capital needs, and debt financing requirements.

The FCFE/FCFF framework is analogous to the DDM framework. The main difference is that now we must be very careful to correctly calculate FCFF and FCFE from the income statement or the statement of cash flows, and we must make sure that we are using the correct discount rate (use the equity cost of capital with FCFE and the WACC with the FCFF).

Use the FCF model instead of DDM if the following conditions apply:

- The firm does not pay cash dividends.
- Dividend policy does not reflect the firm's long-run profitability.
- The firm is a take-over target (because FCF models take a control perspective).

Free Cash Flow to the Firm

There are four definitions for FCFF depending on the data given. Unfortunately, we are going to advise you to know all four (if that's just too much, then you should concentrate on the first and the last). Assuming that the only noncash charge is depreciation, the four definitions are as follows:

FCFF from NI: FCFF = NI + dep + [interest × (1 – tax rate)] – FCInv –WCInv

FCFF from EBIT: FCFF = [EBIT × (1 – tax rate)] + dep – FCInv – WCInv

FCFF from EBITDA: FCFF = [EBITDA × (1 – tax rate)]+ (dep × tax rate) – FCInv – WCInv

FCFF from CFO: FCFF = CFO + [interest × (1 – tax rate)] – FCInv

where:
FCInv = net investment in fixed capital (commonly called capex)
WCInv = net investment in working capital (excluding cash)
EBITDA = earnings before interest, taxes, depreciation, and amortization

Free Cash Flow to Equity

We have four formulas for calculating FCFE:

FCFE from FCFF: FCFE = FCFF – [interest × (1 – tax rate)]+ net borrowing

FCFE from NI: FCFE = NI + dep – FCInv – WCInv + net borrowing

FCFE from CFO: FCFE = CFO – FCInv + net borrowing

FCFE with target debt ratio: FCFE = NI – [(1 – DR) × (FCInv – dep)] – [(1 – DR) × WCInv]

In the last version, DR stands for the constant debt ratio. It is *imperative* that you know how to calculate FCFF and FCFE. This looks like a formidable task (and it is), but if you look at the accounting relationships you'll see that there is a lot of overlap between the formulas. Also, note that you use these formulas to calculate FCFF and FCFE given the accounting inputs.

Dividends, share repurchases, and share issues have no effect on FCFF and FCFE; leverage changes have only a minor effect on FCFE and no effect on FCFF.

If you have to *forecast* FCFF or FCFE, there are two ways to proceed:

1. First, you could calculate FCFF or FCFE for a base year and then apply a growth rate to the calculated value.

2. Alternatively, you could separately forecast each component of the FCFF or FCFE calculation.

Single-Stage FCFF/FCFE Models

Valuation using FCFF and FCFE is very similar to valuation using the DDMs. Let's begin with single-stage valuation. The formulas (which should look familiar) are as follows:

$$\text{For FCFF valuation: firm value} = \frac{\text{FCFF}_1}{\text{WACC} - g}$$

$$\text{For FCFE valuation: equity value} = \frac{\text{FCFE}_1}{\text{required return on equity} - g}$$

Note that to find the value of the firm today, the numerator is next year's FCF (i.e., FCFF_1 and FCFE_1). *It is imperative that you use the correct discount rate with the correct formula.* Since the FCFF framework values the entire firm, the cost of capital from all sources must be used (i.e., WACC). FCFE values only the cash flows that belong to equity holders; hence, the equity discount rate, *r*, is appropriate (think CAPM).

Two-Stage FCFF/FCFE Models

The 2-stage FCF framework is also analogous to the 2-stage DDM framework.

Remember the following steps:

Step 1: Chart the FCFs in high-growth period.
Step 2: Use single-stage FCF model to calculate terminal value at end of high-growth period.
Step 3: Discount interim FCF and terminal value to time zero to find value; use WACC with FCFF to find firm value; use required return on equity with FCFE to find equity value.

Professor's Note: The guiding principle behind DCF valuation is that the value of the security is simply the discounted value of all future cash flows.

Market-Based Valuation: Price Multiples

Cross-Reference to CFA Institute Assigned Topic Review #35

Price multiples are ratios of a common stock's market price to some fundamental variable. The most common example is the price-to-earnings (P/E) ratio. A **justified price multiple** is what the multiple *should be* if the stock is fairly valued. If the actual multiple is greater than the justified price multiple, the stock is overvalued; if the actual multiple is less than the justified multiple, the stock is undervalued (all else equal).

A price multiple can be justified based on one of two methods:

1. The justified price multiple for the **method of comparables** is an average multiple of similar stocks in the same peer group. The economic rationale for the method of comparables is the Law of One Price, which asserts that two similar assets should sell at comparable prices (i.e., multiples).

2. The justified price multiple for the **method of forecasted fundamentals** is the ratio of the value of the stock from a discounted cash flow (DCF) valuation model divided by some fundamental variable (e.g., earnings per share). The economic rationale for the method of forecasted fundamentals is that the value used in the numerator of the justified price multiple is derived from a DCF model that is based on the most basic concept in finance: value is equal to the present value of expected future cash flows discounted at the appropriate risk-adjusted rate of return.

The Price-to-Earnings (P/E) Ratio

The most common market multiple is the P/E ratio. The main argument in favor of P/E valuation is that earnings power, as measured by EPS, is the primary determinant of investment value. There are a few problems with using the P/E ratio as a valuation tool:

- Earnings can be negative, which makes the P/E meaningless.
- The volatile, transitory portion of earnings makes the interpretation of P/Es difficult for analysts.
- Management has considerable discretion over accounting choices that affect reported earnings.

The P/E ratio can be calculated on a *leading* or *trailing basis*. On a trailing basis, earnings over the last 12 months are used in the denominator. With a leading basis, next year's expected earnings are used in the denominator.

While the price is always the market price of a share of stock, the analyst must determine the EPS. Analysts frequently use normalized EPS rather than EPS from the most recent financial statements. There are two methods of normalization:

1. *Historical average EPS.* The EPS in the P/E ratio is the historical average from the most recent complete business cycle.
2. *Average ROE.* The EPS in the P/E ratio is the average ROE over the most recent complete business cycle times the current book value per share.

On the exam, you are most likely to be presented with a market multiple valuation question dealing with forecasted fundamentals (as opposed to the comparison sample method). In all cases we present here, *the "forecasted fundamentals method" is economics-talk for rearranging the DCF formulas to solve for the desired market-multiple relationship.* In most cases, this involves rearranging (and substituting into) the Gordon model. For the P/E ratio, if you substitute and rearrange, you get the formulas for the forecasted fundamental P/E ratio:

$$\text{justified leading P/E} = \frac{P_0}{E_1} = \frac{1-b}{r-g}$$

$$\text{justified trailing P/E} = \frac{P_0}{E_0} = \frac{(1-b)(1+g)}{r-g}$$

In both formulas, *b* is the retention ratio [so (1 – b) is the payout ratio]. You should be able to determine how changes in the variables in the formula impact the justified P/E. All else equal, the higher the required rate of return, the lower the P/E will be; the higher the growth rate, the higher the P/E will be.

The PEG Ratio

The PEG ratio is equal to the ratio of the P/E multiple to earnings growth:

$$\text{PEG ratio} = \frac{P/E}{g}$$

The implied valuation rule is that stocks with lower PEG ratios are undervalued relative to high-PEG stocks, assuming similar risk.

The Price-to-Book (P/B) Ratio

The P/B ratio is calculated as the market price per share divided by the book value per share (common stockholders' equity = total assets – total liabilities – preferred stock). The *advantages* of the P/B ratio include the following:

- Book value is usually positive, even when earnings are negative.

- Book value is more stable than EPS.
- Book value is an appropriate measure of net asset value (especially for firms such as financial institutions that hold liquid assets).

The *disadvantages* of the P/B ratio include the following:

- P/Bs can be misleading when there are significant size differences between firms.
- Book value is influenced by accounting choices/conventions.
- Inflation and technology can cause the book value and the market value of assets to differ significantly.

As with the P/E ratio, if we substitute into and rearrange the Gordon model, we can obtain a formula for the justified P/B:

$$\text{justified P/B} = \frac{\text{ROE} - \text{g}}{\text{r} - \text{g}}$$

The P/B increases as ROE increases. It also increases as the spread between ROE and *r* increases. Common adjustments to the book value include the exclusion of intangible assets such as goodwill. Since the book value forecasts are not widely disseminated like EPS forecasts, analysts typically use trailing book value when calculating P/Bs.

The Price-to-Sales (P/S) Ratio

The P/S ratio is calculated by dividing the firm's stock price by revenue per share. The *advantages* of the P/S ratio include the following:

- The ratio is meaningful even for distressed firms.
- Sales revenue is not easily manipulated.
- P/S ratios are not as volatile as P/E ratios.
- P/S ratios are particularly useful in valuing mature, cyclical, and zero-income (start-up) firms.

The *disadvantages* of using the P/S ratio include the following:

- High sales do not necessarily mean high profits or cash flows.
- The P/S ratio does not capture differences in the cost structure between firms.
- Revenue recognition practices still distort sales.

Allowing PM_0 to denote the trailing profit margin (defined as NI/sales), we can substitute into and rearrange the Gordon model to get the formula for the justified P/S ratio:

$$\text{justified P/S ratio} = \frac{\left(E_0 / S_0\right) \times (1-b) \times (1+g)}{r-g}$$

$$= \text{net profit margin} \times \text{justified trailing P/E}$$

The P/S increases as the profit margin increases and as growth increases. The P/S ratio is usually calculated using trailing sales.

Price-to-Cash-Flow Ratios

Since value depends largely on the ability of the firm to generate cash, price-to-cash-flow multiples make intuitive sense. The *advantages* of using price-to-cash-flow multiples include the following:

- Cash flow is more difficult for managers to manipulate.
- Price-to-cash-flow is more stable than P/E.
- Price-to-cash-flow mitigates many concerns about the quality of reported earnings.

The *disadvantages* of price-to-cash-flow multiples include the following:

- Determining true cash flow from operations may be difficult.
- FCFE may be better than cash flow to the entire firm, but it's also more volatile.

But which measure of cash flow do we use? There are several cash flow measures with which you should be familiar:

- *Price-to-cash-flow (P/CF):* CF = NI + depreciation + amortization.
- *Price-to-adjusted CFO (P/CFO):* adjusted CFO = CFO + [(net cash interest outflow) × (1 – tax rate)].
- *Price-to-FCFE:* FCFE = CFO – FCInv + net borrowing.
- *Price-to-EBITDA:* EBITDA = earnings before interest, taxes, depreciation, and amortization.

Theoretically, FCFE is the preferred way to define cash flow. However, FCFE is also more volatile than traditional cash flow. EBITDA is a measure of cash flow to all providers of capital (i.e., both debt and equity). Hence, it may be better suited to valuing the entire firm rather than just the equity stake. Analysts typically use trailing cash flows when calculating price-to-cash-flow ratios.

Methods of Comparables

The basic idea of the method of comparables is to compare a stock's price multiple to the benchmark. *Firms with multiples below the benchmark are undervalued, and firms with multiples above the benchmark are overvalued.*

However, the fundamentals of the stock should be similar to the fundamentals of the benchmark before we can make direct comparisons and draw any conclusions about whether the stock is overvalued or undervalued. In other words, we have to ensure that we're comparing apples to apples (sorry for the cliché). That's why the fundamental variables (i.e., the fundamentals) that affect each multiple are important in applying the method of comparables.

Residual Income Valuation

Cross-Reference to CFA Institute Assigned Topic Review #36

Residual income, or economic profit, is equal to the net income of a firm less a charge that measures stockholders' opportunity costs in generating that income. That is, residual income recognizes that accounting profits actually overstate economic profit since the cost of the capital committed to the firm is not included in the calculation of accounting profit (note the similarities to our discussion of EVA®). Residual income is calculated as follows:

RI = net income – equity charge

where:
equity charge = equity capital × cost of equity

Residual Income Model Valuation

The residual income model can be used in a valuation setting. Residual income breaks the firm value into two components:

1. Adjusted current book value of equity.

2. Present value of expected future RI.

Under the residual income model, the intrinsic value of the stock can be expressed as follows:

$$V_0 = B_0 + \left\{ \frac{RI_1}{(1+r)^1} + \frac{RI_2}{(1+r)^2} + \frac{RI_3}{(1+r)^3} + \ldots \right\}$$

where:
B_0 = current book value
$RI_t = E_t - (r \times B_{t-1}) = (ROE - r)(B_{t-1})$
r = required return on equity
ROE = expected return on new investments (expected return on equity)

The *single-stage residual income model* assumes residual income grows at a constant rate (*g*) which is less than the required return on equity (*r*).

$$V_0 = B_0 + \left[\frac{(ROE - r) \times B_0}{r - g} \right]$$

Strengths and Weaknesses of the Residual Income Approach

The *strengths* of the residual income approach include the following:

- Terminal value does not dominate the valuation equation (as with DDM and FCFE approaches).
- Residual income uses available accounting data.
- Residual income is applicable to non-dividend-paying firms.
- Residual income focuses on economic profits.

The *limitations* of the residual income approach are as follows:

- The accounting data may be manipulated by management.
- The accounting data may require significant adjustment.
- The model assumes a clean surplus relationship (i.e., ending BV = beginning BV + earnings – dividends).

The model is most appropriate for non-dividend paying firms, firms with negative FCF for the foreseeable future, or firms with high uncertainty about the terminal value of the equity.

Accounting Issues

There are many accounting issues associated with the residual income approach. Any accounting procedure that results in a direct charge to equity (e.g., foreign currency translation adjustments and some pension adjustments, etc.) will cause the residual income approach to break down. If the residual income model shows up on the exam, the most likely accounting issues that you will have to deal with involve balance sheet adjustments. Common balance sheet adjustments that you may have to allow for include the following:

- Changing inventory value from LIFO to current value.
- Capitalization of operating leases.
- Pension asset/liability issues.
- Goodwill.

On the exam, make the adjustments to the balance sheet and then calculate the value of the stock with the residual income method.

Multistage Residual Income Model

To implement a multistage residual income model, forecast residual income over a short-term, high-growth horizon (e.g., five years) and then make some simplifying assumptions about the pattern of residual income growth over the long term after the high-growth phase. *Continuing residual income* is the residual income that is expected over the long term. In the multistage residual income model, intrinsic value is the sum of three components:

$$V_0 = B_0 + (\text{PV of interim high-growth RI}) + (\text{PV of continuing residual income})$$

Continuing residual income will continue beyond a specified earnings horizon depending on the fortunes of the industry, as well as on the sustainability of a specific firm's competitive prospects over the longer term. The projected rate at which residual income is expected to fade over the life cycle of the firm is captured by a persistence factor, which is between zero and one.

To simplify the model, we typically make one of the following assumptions about continuing residual income over the long term:

- Residual income is expected to persist at its current level forever.
- Residual income is expected to drop immediately to zero.
- Residual income is expected to decline to a long-run average level consistent with a mature industry.
- Residual income is expected to decline over time as ROE falls to the cost of equity (in which case residual income is eventually zero).

An analysis of the firm's position in its industry and the structure of the industry will be necessary to justify one of these assumptions. The third scenario is the most realistic if we assume that over time industry competition reduces economic profits to the point at which firms begin to leave the industry and ROE stabilizes at a long-run normal level. The strength of the persistence factor will depend partly on the sustainability of the firm's competitive advantage and the structure of the industry: the more sustainable the competitive advantage and the better the industry prospects, the higher the persistence factor.

Private Company Valuation

Cross-Reference to CFA Institute Assigned Topic Review #37

Private firms include sole proprietorships and privately held corporations (not publicly traded). Valuation of private firms is based on some of the same company-specific factors which influence the value of publicly traded firms, such as:

- Stage of lifecycle.
- Firm size.
- Influence of short term investors.
- Quality and depth of management.
- Management/shareholder overlap.
- Quality of financial and other information.
- Taxes.

The stock of private firms, however, will typically have less liquidity and more restrictions on marketability than publicly traded shares. Private firms also typically have more concentrated ownership of its equity.

Reasons for Valuing the Total Capital of Private Companies

There are three primary reasons for valuing the total capital and/or equity capital of private companies: (1) transaction-related valuations, (2) compliance-related valuations, and (3) litigation-related valuations.

Transaction-related valuations are necessary when selling or financing a firm.

- Venture capital financing.
- Initial public offering (IPO).
- Sale in an acquisition.
- Bankruptcy proceedings.
- Performance-based managerial compensation.

Compliance-related valuations are performed for legal or regulatory reasons and primarily focus on financial reporting and tax issues.

Litigation-related valuations may be required for shareholder suits, damage claims, lost profits claims, or divorce settlements.

The appropriate valuation method depends on what the valuation will be used for and whether the firm is a going concern. Alternative **definitions of value** include:

- Fair market value.
- Fair value for financial reporting.
- Fair value for litigation.
- Market value.
- Investment value.
- Intrinsic value.

Approaches to Private Company Valuation

- *Income approach:* Values a firm as the present value of its expected future income. Such valuation has many valuations and may be based on a variety of different assumptions.
- *Market approach:* Values a firm using the price multiples based on recent sales of comparable assets.
- *Asset-based approach:* Values a firm's assets minus its liabilities.

Estimating Normalized Earnings

Normalized earnings should exclude nonrecurring and unusual items. In the case of private firms with a concentrated control, there may be discretionary or tax-motivated expenses, excessive compensation, or payment of personal expenses by the firm that require adjustment when estimating normalized earnings. Many analysts also adjust for company-owned real estate, removing the revenues and expenses of the real estate from the income statement and putting in a market-based estimate of rental cost of real estate used in the company's operations. The value of the real estate is then added to the income-based value of the firm as if owned real estate is all a non-operating asset of the firm. These adjustments can be quite significant when the firm is small.

Strategic and Nonstrategic Buyers

A transaction may be either strategic or financial (nonstrategic). In a strategic transaction, valuation of the firm is based in part on the perceived synergies of the target with the acquirer's other assets. A financial transaction assumes no synergies, as when one firm buys another in a dissimilar industry.

Discount Rate Estimation

Estimating the discount rate in a private firm valuation can be quite challenging for the following reasons.

- *Size premiums:* Size premiums are often added to the discount rates for small private companies. Estimating this premium using small public firm data may be biased upward by the fact many of the small firms in the sample are experiencing financial distress.
- *Availability and cost of debt:* A private firm may have less access to debt financing than a public firm. Because equity capital is usually more expensive than debt and because the higher operating risk of smaller private companies results in a higher cost of debt as well, WACC will typically be higher for private firms.
- *Acquirer versus target:* When acquiring a private firm, some acquirers will incorrectly use their own (lower) cost of capital, rather than the higher rate appropriate for the target, and arrive at a value for the target company that is too high.
- *Projection risk:* Because of the lower availability of information from private firms and managers who are inexperienced at forecasting, that analyst should increase the discount rate used.
- Management may not be experienced with forecasting and may underestimate or overestimate future earnings, requiring adjustment by the analyst. Such adjustments are highly subjective, however.
- *Lifecycle stage:* It is particularly difficult to estimate the discount rate for firms in an early stage of development. If such firms have unusually high levels of unsystematic risk, the use of the CAPM may be inappropriate. Although ranges of discount rates can be specified for the various lifecycle stages, it may difficult to classify the stage a firm is in.

CAPM Limitations

Using the CAPM, the expanded CAPM, and build-up methods to estimate discount rates for private firms may not be as straightforward as that for public firms.

- *CAPM:* Typically, beta is estimated from public firm data, and this may not be appropriate for private firms that have little chance of going public or being acquired by a public firm. Due to the differences between large public firms and small private firms, some U.S. tax courts have rejected the use of the CAPM for private firms.
- *Expanded CAPM:* This version of the CAPM includes additional premiums for size and firm-specific (unsystematic) risk.

- *Build-up method:* When it is not possible to find comparable public firms for beta estimation, the build-up method can be used. Beginning with the expected return on the market (beta is implicitly assumed to be one), premiums are added for small size, industry factors, and company specific factors.

Market Approaches to Valuation

- The *guideline public company method* uses the market values of similar publicly traded shares adjusted for differences in growth and risk between the two companies.
- The *guideline transactions method* uses the values from actual sales of controlling positions in either public or private companies.
- The *prior transaction method* uses sales prices from actual transactions in the subject company's shares.

Asset-Based Approaches to Valuation

The asset-based approach estimates the value of firm equity as the fair value of its assets minus the fair value of its liabilities. It is generally not used for going concerns.

Control and Marketability

A controlling equity position is regarded as more valuable than a minority position, as it gives the owner the ability to determine company strategy and dividend policy. Shares that are more marketable (liquid) are more valuable than otherwise identical, less marketable shares.

When estimating share values relative to market or transactions prices for similar shares, adjustment must be made for differences in control and marketability. For example, comparable values are for publicly traded shares, should be reduced by a discount for lack of marketability. The size of a marketability discount can be estimated using the difference between the sales price of traded shares and restricted shares of the same company or the difference between pre-IPO and post-IPO sales prices of shares.

On the other hand, if the comparable value is for publicly traded shares (a minority position) and the analyst is valuing a controlling interest in a private company, he would add a control premium to the comparable's value. Of course, if the comparable value is for a controlling position and the analyst is valuing a minority position, a discount for lack of control would be appropriate.

Alternative Investments

Study Session 13

Topic Weight on Exam	5–15%
SchweserNotes™ Reference	Book 4, Pages 9–135

Private Real Estate Investments

Cross-Reference to CFA Institute Assigned Topic Review #38

Real Estate Investments

Figure 1 shows types of real estate investments.

Figure 1: Basic Forms of Real Estate Investment

	Debt	*Equity*
Private	Mortgages	Direct investments such as sole ownership, partnerships, and commingled funds
Public	Mortgage-backed securities	Shares of REITs and REOCs

Reasons to Invest in Real Estate and Risks of Investing

Reasons to invest in real estate include generation of current income and capital appreciation, as an inflation hedge, for portfolio diversification, and for tax benefits.

Principal risks of investing in real estate include the influence of business conditions on valuation, lead time in developing new property, cost and availability of capital, unexpected inflation, influence of demographic factors, lack of liquidity, environmental issues, lack of information, need for management expertise, and the use of leverage.

Real Estate Valuation

Appraisers use three different approaches to value real estate: the cost approach, the income approach, and the sales comparison approach.

1. The Cost Approach to Valuation

Under the *cost approach*, a value is derived by adding the value of the land to the current replacement cost of a new building less adjustments for estimated depreciation and obsolescence. The steps involved with applying the cost approach are:

1. Estimate the market value of the land.

2. Estimate the building's replacement cost.

3. Deduct depreciation including physical deterioration, functional obsolescence, locational obsolescence, and economic obsolescence.

The cost approach is most useful 1) when the subject property is relatively new, 2) for unusual properties, or 3) for properties where comparable transactions are limited.

2. The Income Approach to Valuation

The *income approach* includes two different valuation methods: the **direct capitalization method** and the **discounted cash flow method**. With the *direct capitalization method*, value is based on capitalizing the first-year net operating income (NOI) of the property using a *capitalization (cap) rate*. With the *discounted cash flow method*, value is based on the present value of the property's future cash flows using an appropriate discount rate.

Net operating income (NOI) is the amount of income remaining after subtracting vacancy and collection losses, as well as operating expenses such as insurance, property taxes, utilities, maintenance, and repairs, from potential gross income. NOI is calculated before subtracting financing costs and income taxes.

If the NOI and value are expected to grow at a constant rate, the cap rate is lower than the discount rate:

$$\text{cap rate} = \text{discount rate} - \text{growth rate}$$

Cap rate is used to capitalize first-year NOI as follows:

$$\text{value} = V_0 = \frac{NOI_1}{\text{cap rate}}$$

Cap rate can also be estimated from comparables:

$$\text{cap rate} = \frac{\text{NOI}_1}{\text{comparable sales price}}$$

Example: Valuation using the direct capitalization method

Suppose the net operating income of an office building is expected to be \$175,000 and the cap rate is 8%. **Estimate** the market value of the property using the direct capitalization method.

Answer:

The estimated market value is:

$$V_0 = \frac{\text{NOI}_1}{\text{cap rate}} = \frac{\$175{,}000}{8\%} = \$2{,}187{,}500$$

The gross income multiplier, another form of direct capitalization, is the ratio of the sales price to the property's expected gross income in the year after purchase. The gross income multiplier can be derived from comparable transactions.

$$\text{gross income multiplier} = \frac{\text{sales price}}{\text{gross income}}$$

Once we obtain the gross income multiplier, value is estimated as a multiple of a subject property's estimated gross income as follows:

$$\text{value} = \text{gross income} \times \text{gross income multiplier}$$

Using the discounted cash flow (DCF) method, investors usually project NOI for a specific holding period, plus the property value at the end of the holding period (i.e., terminal value). Terminal value can be estimated by capitalizing future NOI at a future cap rate known as the *terminal* or *residual cap rate.* The terminal cap rate may be different from the "*going-in*" (initial) *cap rate.*

When tenants are required to pay all expenses, a cap rate may be applied to rent instead of to NOI. The cap rate that results from dividing rent by comparable sales is called the *all risks yield* (ARY).

Valuation With Different Lease Structures

Lease structures can vary by country. Adjustments must be made when the contract rent (i.e., passing or term rent) and the current market rent (i.e., open market rent) differ. When the lease is renewed, rent is likely to be adjusted to the current market rent.

One way of dealing with the expected change in rent is the *term and reversion approach,* whereby the contract (term) rent and the reversion are appraised separately using different cap rates. The *reversion cap rate* is derived from comparable, fully let, properties. Because the reversion occurs in the future, it must be discounted to the present. The discount rate applied to the contract rent is likely to be lower than the reversion rate because the contract rent is less risky (i.e., the existing tenants are less likely to default on a below-market lease).

A variation of the term and reversion approach is the *layer method.* With the layer method, one source (layer) of income is the contract (term) rent that is assumed to continue in perpetuity. The second layer is the increase in rent that occurs when the lease expires and the rent is reviewed. A cap rate similar to the all risks yield is applied to the term rent because the term rent is less risky. A higher cap rate is applied to the incremental income that occurs as a result of the rent review.

3. The Sales Comparison Approach to Valuation

Under the *sales comparison approach,* the sales prices of similar (comparable) properties are adjusted for differences from the subject property. The differences may relate to size, age, location, property condition, and market conditions at the time of sale. The values of comparable transactions are adjusted upward (downward) for undesirable (desirable) differences with the subject property.

Example: Sales comparison approach

An appraiser has been asked to estimate the value of a warehouse and has collected the following information:

		Comparable Transactions		
Unit of Comparison	*Subject Property*	*1*	*2*	*3*
Size, in square feet	30,000	40,000	20,000	35,000
Age, in years	5	9	4	5
Physical condition	Average	Good	Average	Poor
Location	Prime	Prime	Secondary	Prime
Sale date, months ago		6	18	12
Sales price		$9,000,000	$4,500,000	$8,000,000

The appraiser's adjustments are based on the following:

- Each adjustment is based on the unadjusted sales price of the comparable.
- Properties depreciate at 2% per annum. Since comparable #1 is 4 years older than the subject, an upward adjustment of $720,000 is made [$9,000,000 × 2% × 4 years].
- Condition adjustment: Good: +5%, average: none; poor: –5%. Since comparable #1 is in better condition than the subject, a downward adjustment of $450,000 is made [$9,000,000 × 5%]. Similarly, an upward adjustment is made for comparable #3 to the tune of $400,000 [$8,000,000 × 5%].
- Location adjustment: Prime: none; secondary: 10%. Since both comparable #1 and the subject are in a prime location, no adjustment is made.
- Over the past 24 months, sales prices have been appreciating 0.5% per month. Since comparable #1 was sold six months ago, an upward adjustment of $270,000 is made [$9,000,000 × 0.5% × 6 months].

Answer:

Once the adjustments are made for all of the comparable transactions, the adjusted sales price per square foot of the comparable transactions are averaged and applied to the subject property as follows:

		Comparable Transactions		
Adjustments	*Subject Property*	*1*	*2*	*3*
Sales price		$9,000,000	$4,500,000	$8,000,000
Age		+720,000	–90,000	—
Condition		–450,000	—	+400,000
Location		—	+450,000	—
Sale date		+270,000	+405,000	+480,000
Adjusted sales price		$9,540,000	$5,265,000	$8,880,000
Size in square feet	30,000	40,000	20,000	35,000
Adjusted sales price per SF		$238.50	$263.25	$253.71
Average sales price per SF	$251.82			
Estimated value	$7,554,600			

Financial Ratios in Real Estate Lending/Investing

Lenders often use the *debt service coverage ratio* (DSCR) and the *loan-to-value* (LTV) ratio to determine the maximum loan amount on a specific property. The maximum loan amount is based on the measure that results in the lowest debt.

The DSCR is calculated as follows:

$$\text{DSCR} = \frac{\text{first year NOI}}{\text{debt services}}$$

The LTV ratio is calculated as follows:

$$\text{LTV} = \frac{\text{loan amount}}{\text{appraised value}}$$

When debt is used to finance real estate, equity investors often calculate the *equity dividend rate*, also known as the cash-on-cash return, which measures the cash return on the amount of cash invested.

$$\text{equity dividend rate} = \frac{\text{first year cash flow}}{\text{equity}}$$

The equity dividend rate only covers one period. It is not the same as the IRR that measures the return over the entire holding period.

Publicly Traded Real Estate Securities

Cross-Reference to CFA Institute Assigned Topic Review #39

Publicly traded real estate securities can take several forms. The main types are real estate investment trusts (REITs), real estate operating companies (REOCs), and residential or commercial mortgage-backed securities (MBS).

Advantages/Disadvantages of Investing in Publicly Traded Real Estate Securities

- Advantages of investing in publicly traded real estate securities include superior liquidity, lower minimum investment, access to premium properties, active professional management, protections afforded to publicly traded securities, and greater diversification potential.
- Advantages of investing in REITs (but not REOCs) include exemption from corporate taxation, predictable earnings, and higher yield.
- Disadvantages of investing in publicly traded real estate securities include lower tax efficiency compared to direct ownership, lack of control, costs of a publicly traded corporate structure, volatility associated with market pricing, limited potential for income growth, forced equity issuance, and structural conflicts of interests.

Due Diligence Considerations of REITs

REIT investors need to pay special attention to:

- Remaining lease terms.
- Inflation protection.
- In-place rents versus market rents.
- Costs to re-lease space.
- Tenant concentration in the portfolio.
- Tenants' financial health.
- New competition.

- Balance sheet analysis.
- Quality of management.

Figure 2: Characteristics of REIT Property Subtypes

	Characteristic			
REIT Type	*Economic Value Determinant*	*Investment Characteristics*	*Principal Risks*	*Due Diligence Considerations*
Shopping/ Retail	1) Retail sales growth 2) Job creation	Stable revenue stream over the short term	Depends on consumer spending	Per-square-foot sales and rental rates
Office	1) Job creation 2) New space supply vs. demand	• Long (5–25 year) lease terms • Stable year-to-year income	Changes in office vacancy and rental rates	• New space under construction • Quality of office space (location, condition of building, etc.)
Residential	1) Population growth 2) Job creation	• One-year leases • Stable	• Competition • Inducements • Regional economy • Inflation of operating costs	• Demographics and income trends • Age and competitive appeal • Cost of home ownership • Rent controls
Health care	1) Population growth 2) New space supply vs. demand	• REITs lease facilities to health care providers • Leases are usually net leases	• Demographics • Government funding • Construction cycles • Financial condition of operators • Tenant litigation	• Operating trends • Government funding trends • Litigation settlements • Insurance costs • Competitors' new facilities vs. demand

Figure 2: Characteristics of REIT Property Subtypes (continued)

	Characteristic			
REIT Type	*Economic Value Determinant*	*Investment Characteristics*	*Principal Risks*	*Due Diligence Considerations*
Industrial	1) Retail sales growth 2) Population growth	• Less cyclical than some other REIT types • 5–25-year net leases • Change in income and values are slow	Shifts in the composition of local and national industrial bases and trade	• Trends in tenants' requirements • Obsolescence of existing space • Need for new types of space • Proximity to transportation • Trends in local supply and demand
Hotel	1) Job creation 2) New space supply vs. demand	• Variable income • Sector is cyclical because it is not protected by long-term leases	• Exposed to business-cycle • Changes in business and leisure travel • Exposure to travel disruptions	• Occupancy, room rates, and operating profit margins vs. industry averages • RevPAR • Trends in forward bookings • Maintenance expenditures • New construction in local markets • Financial leverage
Storage	1) Population growth 2) Job creation	Space is rented under gross leases and on a monthly basis	Ease of entry can lead to overbuilding	• Construction of new competitive facilities • Trends in housing sales • Demographic trends • New business start-up activity • Seasonal trends in demand for storage facilities (can be significant in some markets)

Approaches to REIT Valuation

1. **Net asset value per share:** NAVPS is based on market values and is considered to be the fundamental measure of value for REITs and REOCs.

   NAVPS is the (per share) amount by which assets exceed liabilities, using current market values rather than accounting book values. The current market values for real estate assets are measured by capitalizing NOI (as discussed earlier) or by using a multiple. The market values of other assets and liabilities are assumed to be equal to their book values.

2. **Relative value:** REITs and REOCs can be valued using market-based approaches by applying a multiple to a property's *funds from operations* (FFO) or *adjusted funds from operations* (AFFO).

   Funds from operations: FFO adjusts reported earnings and is a popular measure of the continuing operating income of a REIT or REOC. FFO is calculated as follows:

   accounting net earnings
   \+ depreciation charges (expenses)
   \+ deferred tax charges (i.e., deferred tax expenses)
   – gains (losses) from sales of property and debt restructuring
   = funds from operations (FFO)

   Price-to-FFO approach:

   funds from operations (FFO)
   ÷ shares outstanding
   = FFO / share
   × sector average P/FFO multiple
   = NAV / share

   Adjusted funds from operations: AFFO is an extension of FFO that is intended to be a more useful representation of current economic income.

   FFO (funds from operations)
   – non-cash (straight-line) rent adjustment
   – recurring maintenance-type capital expenditures and leasing commissions
   = AFFO (adjusted funds from operations)

AFFO is considered a better measure of economic income than FFO because AFFO considers the capital expenditures that are required to sustain the property's economic income. However, FFO is more frequently cited in practice because AFFO relies more on estimates and is considered more subjective.

Price-to-AFFO approach:

funds from operations (FFO)
– non-cash rents
– recurring maintenance-type capital expenditures
= AFFO
÷ shares outstanding
= AFFO / share
× property subsector average P/AFFO multiple
= NAV / share

3. **Discounted cash flow:** Dividend discount models typically include two or three stages, based on near- and long-term growth forecasts. Discounted cash flow models use intermediate-term cash flow projections, plus a terminal value based on historical cash flow multiples.

   value of a REIT share
   = PV(dividends for years 1 through n) + PV(terminal value at the end of year n)

Private Equity

Cross-Reference to CFA Institute Assigned Topic Review #40

Sources of Value Creation

It is commonly believed that PE firms have the ability to add greater value to their portfolio companies than do publicly governed firms. The sources of this increased value are thought to come from the following:

1. The ability to re-engineer the firm and operate it more efficiently.
2. The ability to obtain debt financing on more advantageous terms.
3. Superior alignment of interests between management and private equity ownership.

Control Mechanisms

Private equity firms use a variety of mechanisms to align their interests with those of the managers of portfolio companies. The following contract terms are contained in the term sheet that specifies the terms of the private equity firm's investment.

Compensation: Managers of the portfolio companies receive compensation that is closely linked to the firm's performance.

Tag-along, drag-along clauses: Any time an acquirer acquires control of the company, they must extend the acquisition offer to all shareholders, including firm management.

The term sheet also contains the following provisions that protect the private equity firm by providing it greater control and equity, some of which are triggered by specific events.

Board representation: The private equity firm is ensured control through board representation if the firm experiences a major event such as a takeover, restructuring, initial public offering (IPO), bankruptcy, or liquidation.

Noncompete clauses: Company founders must sign such clauses that prevent them from competing against the firm for a prespecified period of time.

Priority in claims: Private equity firms receive their distributions before other owners, often in the form of preferred dividends. They also have priority on the firm's assets if the portfolio company is liquidated.

Required approvals: Changes of strategic importance (e.g., acquisitions, divestitures, and changes in the business plan) must be approved by the private equity firm.

Earn-outs: These are used predominantly in venture capital investments and tie the acquisition price paid by the private equity firm to the portfolio company's future performance over a specific period.

Appropriate control mechanisms in the investment contract allow private equity firms to make investments in companies of considerable risk.

Valuation Characteristics of Venture Capital vs. Buyout

Figure 3: Valuation Characteristics of Venture Capital and Buyout Investments

Characteristic	*Venture Capital Investments*	*Buyout Investments*
Cash Flows	Low predictability with potentially unrealistic projections	Stable and predictable cash flows
Product Market	New product market with uncertain future	Strong market position, with a possible niche position
Products	Product is based on new technology with uncertain prospects	Established products
Asset Base	Weak	Substantial base that can serve as collateral
Management Team	New team although individual members typically have a strong entrepreneurial record	Strong and experienced
Financial Leverage	Low debt use with a majority of equity financing	High amounts of debt with a large percentage of senior debt and substantial amounts of junior and mezzanine debt
Risk Assessment	Risk is difficult to measure due to new technologies, markets, and firm history	Risk can be measured due to industry and firm maturity
Exit	Exit via IPO or firm sale is difficult to forecast	Exit is predictable
Operations	High cash burn rate required due to firm and product immaturity	Potential exists for reduction in inefficiencies
Working Capital Required	Increasing requirements due to growth	Low requirements
Due Diligence Performed by Private Equity Firms	Private equity firms investigate technological and commercial prospects; investigation of financials is limited due to short history	Private equity firms perform extensive due diligence
Goal Setting	Goals are milestones set in business plan and growth strategy	Goals reference cash flows, strategic plan, and business plan

continued on next page

Figure 3: Valuation Characteristics of Venture Capital and Buyout Investments (continued)

Characteristic	*Venture Capital Investments*	*Buyout Investments*
Private Equity Investment Returns	High returns come from a few highly successful investments with writeoffs from less successful investments	Low variability in the success of investments with failures being rare
Capital Market Presence	Generally not active in capital markets	Active in capital markets
Sales Transactions	Most firms are sold as a result of the relationship between venture capital firm and entrepreneurs	Firms are typically sold in an auction-type process
Ability to grow through subsequent funding	Firms are less scalable as subsequent funding is typically smaller	Strong performers can increase subsequent funding amounts
Source of general partner's variable revenue	Carried interest is most common, transaction and monitoring fees are less common	Carried interest, transaction fees, and monitoring fees

Figure 4: Valuation Issues for Buyouts vs. Venture Capital Investments

Valuation Issue	*Buyout*	*Venture Capital*
Applicability of DCF Method	Frequently used to estimate value of equity	Less frequently used as cash flows are uncertain
Applicability of Relative Value Approach	Used to check the value from DCF analysis	Difficult to use because there may be no true comparable firms
Use of Debt	High	Low as equity is dominant form of financing
Key Drivers of Equity Return	Earnings growth, increase in multiple upon exit, and reduction in the debt	Pre-money valuation, investment, and subsequent dilution

There are four typical **exit routes** for private equity firms: (1) initial public offerings (IPOs), (2) secondary market sales, (3) management buyouts (MBOs), and (4) liquidations.

The general **private equity risk factors** include liquidity risk, unquoted investments risk, competitive environment risk, agency risk, capital risk, regulatory risk, tax risk, valuation risk, diversification risk and market risk.

The **costs of investing in private equity** are significantly higher than with publicly traded securities and include transaction costs, investment vehicle fund setup costs, administrative costs, audit costs, management and performance costs, dilution costs, and placement fees.

Important **economic terms of a private equity fund** include management, transaction fees, carried interest, ratchet, hurdle rate, target fund size, vintage, and the term of the fund.

The **corporate governance terms** in the prospectus provide the legal arrangements for the control of the fund and include key man clauses, performance disclosure and confidentiality, clawback, distribution waterfall, tag-along, drag-along clauses, removal for cause, no-fault divorce, investment restrictions, and co-investment.

Quantitative Measures

The more popular multiples and those specified by GIPS include the following:

PIC (paid-in capital). The percent of committed or absolute amount of capital utilized by the GP to date.

DPI (distributed to paid-in capital). The cumulative distributions paid to the LPs divided by the cumulative invested capital. It is net of management fees and carried interest and is also referred to as the cash-on-cash return.

RVPI (residual value to paid-in capital). This measures the LP's unrealized return and is the value of the LP's holdings in the fund divided by the cumulative invested capital. It is net of management fees and carried interest.

TVPI (total value to paid-in capital). This measures the LP's realized and unrealized return and is the sum of DPI and RVPI. It is net of management fees and carried interest.

The fraction (f) of the firm that a venture capital investor must own as a result of a new investment (single-round) can be calculated as:

$$\text{NPV method: } f = \frac{\text{new investment}}{\text{present value of entire firm value at exit}}$$

$$\text{IRR method: } f = \frac{\text{future value of new investment at exit}}{\text{future value of entire firm value at exit}}$$

These will be equal as long as the discount factor for the NPV method is equal to the rate of growth used for future value in the IRR method.

Investing in Hedge Funds: A Survey

Cross-Reference to CFA Institute Assigned Topic Review #41

This topic review focuses on hedge funds as an asset class and issues that must be addressed while considering inclusion of hedge funds in an investor's portfolio.

Hedge Funds vs. Mutual Funds

Figure 5: Hedge Fund vs. Mutual Fund

	Leverage	*Use of Derivatives*	*Disclosure Requirements*	*Lock-Up Periods*	*Fee Structure*	*Investors*	*Liquidity*
Hedge fund	May be high	May be high	Low	Long	Management & incentive (higher)	Qualified only	Low
Mutual fund	Low	Low—limited	High	Short or none	Management only (lower)	General public	High (daily liquidity)

Hedge Fund Performance Biases

Lack of regulatory requirements for hedge funds to file performance reports leads to voluntary reporting of performance data to index providers. Hedge fund index data suffers from the following:

- Selection bias (better performers are more likely to report).
- Backfill bias (inclusion of the strong historical performance of those funds that initiate reporting).
- Survivorship bias (the historical data of deceased funds is purged).

All three biases lead to artificially inflated average performance.

Factor Models

Regression analysis can be used to separate alpha and beta return in hedge fund performance. This allows investors to evaluate whether hedge fund fees are justified by alpha returns. Factor models should be scrutinized to ensure that there are no omitted factors (which would lead to artificially high measured alpha return).

Non-Normality of Hedge Fund Returns

Hedge fund return distributions are non-normal, and this makes standard deviation an inadequate measure of risk. In the presence of non-normality, positive skewness and low kurtosis are desired attributes for an investor. However, hedge fund return distributions often exhibit negative skewness and high kurtosis.

Mean-Variance Optimization and Hedge Funds

Traditional mean-variance optimization uses the expected return, standard deviation, and correlations of each asset as inputs. Unfortunately, for hedge funds:

- Expected returns are difficult to predict because index data is biased.
- Standard deviation is misleading due to non-normality of hedge fund returns.
- Correlations are dynamic and could change.

As a result, unconstrained mean-variance optimization is likely to lead to a portfolio allocation to hedge funds that is too high; adjustments should be made to avoid this.

Hedge Fund Replication

If the majority of a hedge fund's returns can be explained by exposure to the same market factors that drive returns on conventional investments such as bond or equity indices, then hedge fund performance can be replicated through investments in such assets. By obtaining these exposures through traditional market sources, an investor can overcome some of the limitations of investing in hedge funds, such as the cost and the lack of liquidity, transparency, and alpha.

Funds of Funds

Funds of funds are intermediary funds that make diversified investments across several single-manager hedge funds. Compared to single-manager funds, funds of funds provide diversification, additional due diligence, better liquidity terms, and lower minimum investments. However, funds of funds add an additional layer of fees. Evidence suggests that funds of funds produce returns that are only on-par with the average single-manager fund, however (due to diversification), funds of funds exhibit lower standard deviation.

Fixed Income

Study Sessions 14 & 15

Topic Weight on Exam	5–15%
SchweserNotes™ Reference	Book 4, Pages 136–309

Fundamentals of Credit Analysis

Cross-reference to CFA Institute Assigned Topic Review #42

Credit risk refers to potential losses from the failure of a borrower to make promised payments and has two components: default risk and loss severity. **Default risk** is the probability that a borrower will fail to pay interest or principal when due. **Loss severity** refers to the value (in money or as a percentage) that a bond investor will lose if the issuer defaults.

The **expected loss** is equal to the default risk multiplied by the loss severity. Percentage loss severity is equal to one minus the **recovery rate**, the percentage of a bond's value an investor will receive if the issuer defaults.

Bonds with greater credit risk trade at higher yields than bonds thought to be free of credit risk. The difference in yield between a credit-risky bond and a credit-risk-free bond of similar maturity is called its **yield spread**. Bond prices decrease when their yield spreads increase.

The yield spread also compensates investors for liquidity risk. **Market liquidity risk** is the risk of receiving less than market value when selling bonds and is reflected in their bid-ask spreads. **Downgrade risk** refers to the risk that spreads will increase because the issuer has become less creditworthy so its credit rating is lowered.

The priority of a bond's claim to the issuer's assets and cash flows is referred to as its **seniority ranking**. Secured debt is backed by collateral, while unsecured debt (debentures) is a general claim against the issuer.

All debt securities in the same category have the same priority and are said to rank **pari passu**. Strict priority of claims is not always applied in practice. In a bankruptcy, the court may approve a reorganization plan that does not strictly conform to the priority of claims.

Credit Ratings

Credit rating agencies assign ratings to corporate issuers based on the creditworthiness of their senior unsecured debt ratings, referred to as **corporate family ratings** (CFR), and to individual debt securities, referred to as **corporate credit ratings** (CCR). Higher ratings indicate a lower expected default rate. **Notching** is the practice of assigning different ratings to bonds of the same issuer.

Figure 8 shows ratings scales used by Standard & Poor's, Moody's, and Fitch. Bonds with ratings of Baa3/BBB– or higher are considered **investment grade**. Bonds rated Ba1/BB+ or lower are considered non-investment grade and are often called **high yield bonds** or **junk bonds**.

Figure 1: Credit Rating Categories

(a) Investment grade ratings	
Moody's	*Standard &Poor's, Fitch*
Aaa	AAA
Aa1	AA+
Aa2	AA
Aa3	AA–
A1	A+
A2	A
A3	A–
Baa1	BBB+
Baa2	BBB
Baa3	BBB–

(b) Non-investment grade ratings	
Moody's	*Standard &Poor's, Fitch*
Ba1	BB+
Ba2	BB
Ba3	BB–
B1	B+
B2	B
B3	B–
Caa1	CCC+
Caa2	CCC
Caa3	CCC–
Ca	CC
C	C
C	D

In a holding company structure, a subsidiary's debt covenants may prohibit the transfer of cash or assets to the parent until after the subsidiary's debt is serviced. The parent company's bonds are thus effectively subordinated to the subsidiary's bonds. This is referred to as **structural subordination** and is considered by rating agencies when notching an issue credit rating.

Relying on ratings from credit rating agencies has risks. Credit ratings change over time and ratings mistakes happen. Event risks specific to a company or industry such as natural disasters, acquisitions, and equity buybacks using debt, are difficult to anticipate and therefore not easily captured in credit ratings. Finally, changes in yield spreads and bond prices anticipate ratings changes and reflect expected losses, while ratings are based solely on default risk.

Credit Analysis

One way to represent the key components of credit analysis is by the **four Cs** of credit analysis: **capacity**, **collateral**, **covenants**, and **character**. *Capacity* refers to a corporate borrower's ability repay its debt obligations on time. *Collateral* refers to the value of a borrower's assets. *Covenants* are the terms and conditions the borrowers and lenders have agreed to as part of a bond issue. *Character* refers to management's integrity and its commitment to repay.

Capacity to repay is assessed by examining: (1) industry structure, (2) industry fundamentals, and (3) company fundamentals. Industry structure can be described by Porter's five forces: rivalry among existing competitors, threat of new entrants, threat of substitute products, bargaining power of buyers, and bargaining power of suppliers. Analysis of industry fundamentals focuses on industry cyclicality (more cyclicality indicates greater credit risk) and growth prospects (earnings growth indicates less credit risk). Company fundamentals include competitive position, operating history, management's strategy and execution, and leverage and coverage ratios.

Collateral analysis is more important for less creditworthy companies. The market value of a company's assets can be difficult to observe directly. High depreciation expense relative to capital expenditures may signal that management is not investing sufficiently and the quality of the company's assets may be poor. Some intangible assets that can be sold to generate cash flows, such as patents, are considered high-quality collateral, whereas goodwill is not considered a high-quality, intangible asset.

Bond covenants protect lenders while leaving some operating flexibility to the borrowers to run the company.

Character analysis includes an assessment of management's ability to develop a sound strategy; management's past performance in operating the company without bankruptcies or restructurings; accounting policies and tax strategies that may be hiding problems, such as revenue recognition issues, frequent restatements, and frequently changing auditors; any record of fraud or other legal and regulatory problems; and prior treatment of bondholders, such as benefits to equity holders at the expense of debt holders through debt-financed acquisitions and special dividends.

Financial ratios used in credit analysis

Profit and cash flow metrics commonly used in ratio analysis include earnings before interest, taxes, depreciation, and amortization (EBITDA); funds from operations (FFO), which is net income from continuing operations plus depreciation, amortization, deferred taxes, and noncash items; free cash flow before dividends; and free cash flow after dividends.

Two primary categories of ratios for credit analysis are leverage ratios and coverage ratios. The three most common measures of leverage used by credit analysts are the debt-to-capital ratio, the debt-to-EBITDA ratio, and the FFO-to-debt ratio. The two most commonly used coverage ratios are EBITDA-to-interest and EBIT-to-interest. When calculating ratios, analysts should adjust debt reported on the financial statements by including the firm's obligations, such as underfunded pension plans (net pension liabilities), and off-balance-sheet liabilities, such as operating leases. In general, higher coverage ratios and lower leverage ratios are associated with higher credit quality. A firm's ratios are compared to benchmark ratios in determining its overall credit rating.

Yield Spreads

A bond's yield spread is primarily affected by five interrelated factors: the credit cycle, economic conditions, financial market performance, broker-dealer capital, and general market demand and supply. Yield spreads on lower-quality issues tend to be more volatile than spreads on higher-quality issues.

The return impact of spread changes depends on both the magnitude of a change and the price sensitivity of the bond's value to interest rate changes (i.e., the bond's duration). For small spread changes, the return impact (percentage change in bond price) can be approximated by:

$$\text{return impact} \approx -\text{modified duration} \times \Delta\text{spread}$$

For larger spread changes, incorporating convexity improves the accuracy of return impact measurement. Note that whether to use only half the convexity depends on the convexity measure used.

$$\text{return impact} \approx -\text{modified duration} \times \Delta\text{spread} + \frac{1}{2}\text{convexity} \times (\Delta\text{spread})^2$$

High Yield Debt

Reasons for non-investment grade ratings may include high leverage; unproven operating history; low or negative free cash flow; high sensitivity to business cycles; low confidence in management; unclear competitive advantages; large off-balance-sheet liabilities; or an industry in decline.

Special considerations for high yield bonds include their liquidity, projections of earnings and cash flow, debt structure, corporate structure, and covenants.

High yield issuers' capital structures often include different types of debt with several levels of seniority and hence varying levels of potential loss severity. Companies for which secured bank debt is a high proportion of the capital structure are said to be *top heavy* and have less capacity to borrow from banks in financially stressful periods. When an issuer has multiple layers of debt with a variety of expected recovery rates, a credit analyst should calculate leverage for each level of the debt structure.

Many high-yield companies use a holding company structure; the resulting **structural subordination** can lead to lower recovery rates for the parent company's debt.

Important covenants for high yield debt may include a **change of control put** that gives debt holders the right to require the issuer to buy back debt in the event of an acquisition; restricted payments to equity holders; limitations on liens; and **restricted subsidiaries**. Restricted subsidiaries' cash flows and assets are designated to service the debt of the parent holding company. This benefits creditors of holding companies because their debt is pari passu with the debt of restricted subsidiaries, rather than structurally subordinated.

Sovereign and Municipal Debt

Sovereign debt is issued by national governments. Sovereign credit analysis must assess both the government's *ability* to service debt and its *willingness* to do so. Willingness is important because bondholders usually have no legal recourse if a national government refuses to pay its debts.

A basic framework for evaluating and assigning a credit rating to sovereign debt includes five key areas:

1. *Institutional effectiveness*: Successful policymaking, absence of corruption, and commitment to honor debts.

2. *Economic prospects*: Growth trends, demographics, income per capita, and size of government relative to the private economy.

3. *International investment position*: Foreign reserves, external debt, and the status of the country's currency in international markets.

4. *Fiscal flexibility*: Willingness and ability to increase revenue or cut expenditures to ensure debt service, and trends in debt as a percentage of GDP.

5. *Monetary flexibility*: Ability to use monetary policy for domestic economic objectives (this might be lacking with exchange rate targeting or membership in a monetary union) and credibility and effectiveness of monetary policy.

Credit rating agencies assign each national government a **local currency debt rating** and a **foreign currency debt rating**. Foreign currency debt typically has a higher default rate and a lower credit rating because the government must purchase foreign currency in the open market to make payments. In contrast, local currency debt can be repaid by simply printing more currency. Ratings can differ by as much as two notches for local currency and foreign currency bonds.

Municipal bonds are issued by state and local governments or their agencies. Municipal bonds usually have lower default rates than corporate bonds with the same credit rating. Most municipal bonds can be classified as general obligation bonds or revenue bonds. **General obligation** (GO) **bonds** are unsecured bonds backed by the full faith and credit (taxing power) of the issuer. **Revenue bonds** finance specific projects. Revenue bonds often have higher credit risk than GO bonds because the project is the sole source of funds to service the debt.

Municipal governments' ability to service their general obligation debt depends ultimately on the local economy. Economic factors to assess include employment, trends in per capita income and per capita debt, the tax base, demographics, and ability to attract new jobs. Credit analysts must also observe revenue variability through economic cycles: reliance on tax revenues that are highly variable over an economic cycles indicates higher credit risk. Municipalities may have underfunded long-term obligations such as pension and other post-retirement benefits.

Analysis of revenue bonds requires both analysis of the project and analysis of the financing structure of the project. A key metric for revenue bonds is the **debt service coverage ratio**, which is the ratio of the project's net revenue to the required interest and principal payments on the bonds.

Term Structure and Volatility of Interest Rates

Cross-Reference to CFA Institute Assigned Topic Review #43

The Yield Curve

The *yield curve* is the relationship between interest rates and time to maturity. You can think of the yield curve as the graphical representation of the *term structure of interest rates*. The yield curve takes one of three shapes: (1) normal (upward-sloping), (2) flat, or (3) inverted (downward-sloping).

The yield curve can change in three ways:[1]

1. A *parallel shift* is when all maturities change by the same amount (e.g., if 1-year rates go up 2%, the 25-year rates also go up 2%). Parallel shifts explain 90% of the observed variation in total bond return variance.
2. A *nonparallel shift* occurs when the slope of the yield curve either steepens or flattens. Nonparallel shifts explain about 8.5% of total bond return variance.
3. A *butterfly twist* refers to changes in the "humped" nature of the curve (i.e., the curve twists to become either more or less humped). These curvature changes only explain about 1.5% of total bond return variance.

Swap Rate Curve as Benchmark

The swap rate curve (also known as the LIBOR curve) is the series of swap rates quoted by swap dealers over maturities extending from 2–30 years that reflect only the credit risk of the counterparty, which is usually a bank, so the swap curve is an AA-rated curve, not a default-free curve. The swap rate curve is preferred over a government bond yield curve for use as a benchmark.

Theories of the Term Structure

Term structure theory tries to explain the shape of the yield curve. There are three theories you need to remember: (1) pure expectations, (2) liquidity preference, and (3) preferred habitat.

The *pure* (unbiased) *expectations theory* suggests that forward rates are solely a function of expected future spot rates. In other words, long-term interest rates equal the mean of expected future short-term rates. The major implications of the pure expectations theory include the following:

- If the yield curve is upward-sloping, short-term rates are expected to rise in the future.

1. Empirical results are reported in Robert Litterman and Jose Scheinkman, "Common Factors Affecting Bond Returns," *Journal of Fixed Income* (June 1991), pp.54–61.

- If the curve is downward-sloping, short-term rates are expected to fall in the future.
- A flat yield curve implies the market expects short-term rates to remain constant.

The *liquidity theory of the term structure* addresses the shortcomings of the pure expectations theory by proposing that forward rates reflect investors' expectations of future spot rates plus a liquidity premium to compensate them for exposure to interest-rate risk. Furthermore, the theory suggests that this liquidity premium is positively related to maturity: a 25-year bond has a larger liquidity premium than a 5-year bond.

Therefore, a positive-sloping yield curve may indicate that either the market expects future interest rates to rise or rates are expected to remain constant (or even fall), but the addition of the liquidity premium results in a positive slope.

The *preferred habitat theory* also proposes that forward rates represent expected future spot rates plus a premium, but it *does not* support the view that this premium is directly related to maturity. Instead, the preferred habitat theory suggests that the existence of an imbalance between the supply and demand for funds in a given maturity range will induce lenders and borrowers to shift from their *preferred habitats* (maturity range) to one that has the opposite imbalance. This theory can be used to explain almost any yield curve shape.

Key Rate Duration

Key rate duration is the approximate percentage change in the value of a bond or bond portfolio in response to a 100 basis point change in a key rate, holding all other rates constant. In other words, you can determine the key rate duration for a portfolio by changing one spot rate (say, the 5-year rate) and observing the change in value of the portfolio. Keep in mind that every security or portfolio has a set of key rate durations, one for each key rate. Key rate duration is particularly useful for measuring the effect of a nonparallel shift in the yield curve on a bond portfolio, because the overall portfolio effect is the sum of the individual effects.

Valuing Bonds With Embedded Options

Cross-Reference to CFA Institute Assigned Topic Review #44

This topic review could get complicated. Make sure you have each concept under your belt before you go on to the next one. Focus on (1) the valuation of a callable bond, (2) the interpretation of the OAS, and (3) the convertible bond terminology.

At Level I, you learned how to value an option-free bond by using the theoretical spot rate curve. This involved discounting each cash flow from the bond by the appropriate spot rate. This procedure works fine for bonds whose cash flows do not depend on the level of interest rates. That is, this procedure works fine for option-free bonds. However, the cash flows from bonds with embedded options depend on the level of interest rates. Hence, this simple spot curve valuation is not appropriate for bonds with optionality.

Valuing Option-Free Bonds With Backward Induction

The best way to review this material is with an example. Consider the binomial tree shown in Figure 1 for a 4.0% annual coupon bond with two years remaining until maturity and a market price of $102.20. Starting on the top line, the blocks at each node include the value of the bond, the coupon payment, and the 1-year forward rate at that node. For example, in the up node at the end of Year 1 (1,U) the price is $99.52, the coupon payment is $4, and the 1-year forward rate is 4.5%.

Figure 2: Valuing a 2-Year, 4% Coupon, Option-Free Bond

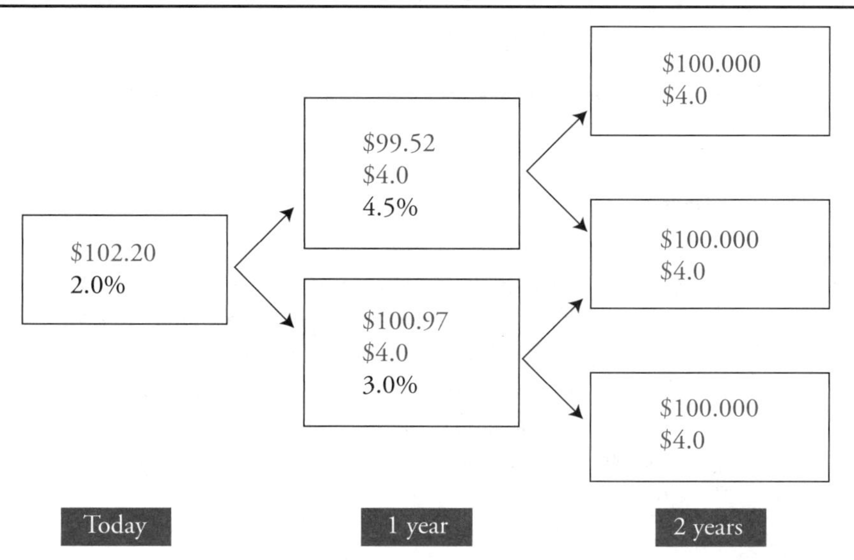

Remember the value of a bond at a given node in a binomial tree is the average of the present values of the two possible values from the next period because the probabilities of an up move and a down move are both 50%. The appropriate discount rate is the forward rate associated with the node under analysis.

Consider the value of the bond at the *upper* node for period 1, $V_{1,U}$:

$$V_{1,U} = \frac{1}{2} \times \left(\frac{\$100 + \$4}{1.045} + \frac{\$100 + \$4}{1.045} \right) = \$99.52$$

Similarly, the value of the bond at the *lower* node for period 1, $V_{1,L}$ is:

$$V_{1,L} = \frac{1}{2} \times \left(\frac{\$100 + \$4}{1.03} + \frac{\$100 + \$4}{1.03} \right) = \$100.97$$

Now calculate V_0, the current value of the bond at node 0:

$$V_0 = \frac{1}{2} \times \left(\frac{\$99.52 + \$4}{1.02} + \frac{\$100.97 + \$4}{1.02} \right) = \$102.20$$

Benchmark Interest Rates

There are three different benchmark interest rates that can be used to calculate spreads:

1. U.S. Treasury Securities.
2. A specific sector of the bond market with a certain credit rating higher than the issue being valued.
3. A specific issuer.

Our interpretation of a spread calculated for a specific security will depend on the benchmark we used.

Callable Bond Valuation

The basic process for valuing a callable bond from an interest rate tree is the same as the process for a noncallable bond. However, when valuing a callable bond, the value used at any node corresponding to the call date and beyond must be either the price at which the issuer will call the bond at that date or the computed value if the bond is not called, *whichever is less*. The price at which the bond will be called is determined using a "call rule," (e.g., the issue will be called if the computed price exceeds 105% of the call price).

Continuing with our example, assume the 2-year bond can be called in one year at 100 and the issuer will call the bond if the call price is less than the computed bond price (i.e., the issuer will call if the price exceeds 100).

Figure 3: Valuing a 2-Year, 4.0% Coupon, Callable Bond, Callable in One Year at 100

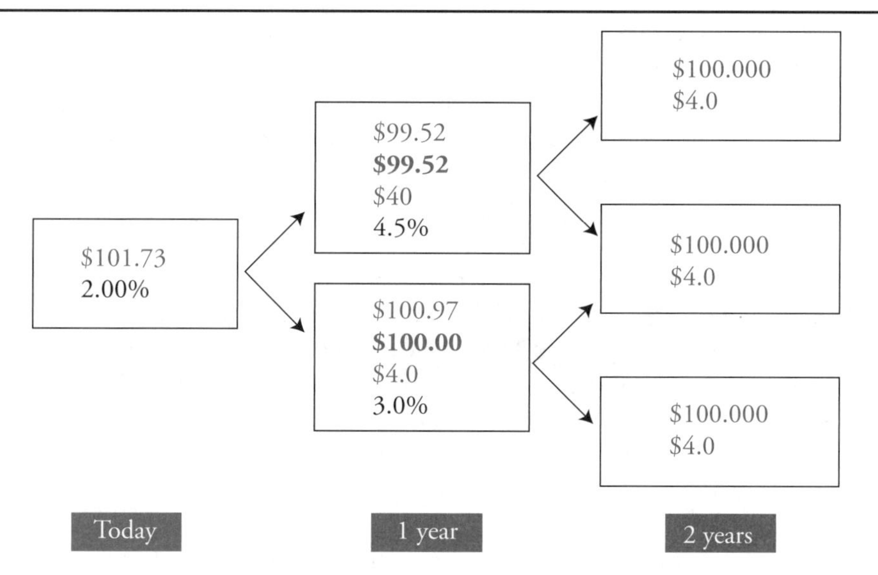

The call rule (call the bond if price exceeds $100) is reflected in the boxes on the tree shown in Figure 2, where the second line of the boxes at the 1-year node (in bold) is the lesser of the call price or the computed value. For example, the value of the bond in one year at the lower node is $100.97. However, in this case the bond will be called, and the investor will only receive $100. Therefore, for valuation purposes, the value of the bond in one year at this node is $100.

The calculation for the current value of the bond at Node 0 (today), assuming the simplified call rules of this example is:

$$V_0 = \frac{1}{2} \times \left(\frac{\$99.52 + \$4}{1.02} + \frac{\$100.00 + \$4}{1.02} \right) = \$101.73$$

Call option value. Using this framework allows us to determine the value of the call option attached to the callable bond. Specifically, the value of the call option is calculated as:

$$V_{call} = V_{noncallable} - V_{callable} = \$102.20 - \$101.73 = \$0.47$$

The formula for an embedded put option is:

$$V_{put} = V_{putable} - V_{nonputable}$$

Option-Adjusted Spread (OAS)

The interest rate tree is typically created to provide an arbitrage-free value for a noncallable Treasury security. If you use the tree to value a callable bond, you will not get a theoretical value that is equal to the market price (the usual case is that the model price will be greater than the market price). In this case, you will want to adjust the interest rates in the tree.

Suppose you can add a constant spread of 50 basis points to the interest rate in every node of the tree. Further, suppose you re-value the callable bond with the "new" interest rates and get a new model value that is equal to the bond's market price. The option-adjusted spread (OAS) is the constant spread that is added to the interest rate in every node of the interest rate tree that forces the model price to be equal to the market price. The OAS is the "spread" over the Treasury securities after removing the option risk from the cash flows. All else equal, you want to buy bonds with big OAS (big OAS implies low price).

Nominal spreads represent differences in yields due to some combination of the following types of risk differences between two bonds: credit risk, liquidity risk, and option risk. OAS removes the option risk component from nominal spreads. In fact, perhaps a better name for the OAS is the "option-removed" spread. What's left is compensation for the difference in credit risk and liquidity risk between the bond of interest and the benchmark security used to create the rates on the tree. If the OAS is larger than required to compensate for credit and liquidity risk, the bond is underpriced. That's why we have to know what benchmark rates were used to create the tree before we can interpret the bond's OAS, as shown in Figure 3.

Figure 4: Relative OAS Valuation

	Treasury Benchmark	*Sector Benchmark*	*Issuer-Specific Benchmark*
OAS > 0	Overvalued ("rich") if actual OAS < required OAS; undervalued ("cheap") if actual OAS > required OAS	Overvalued ("rich") if actual OAS < required OAS; undervalued ("cheap") if actual OAS > required OAS	Undervalued ("cheap")
OAS = 0	Overvalued ("rich")	Overvalued ("rich")	Fairly priced
OAS < 0	Overvalued ("rich")	Overvalued ("rich")	Overvalued ("rich")

Convertible Bonds

Convertible bonds can be converted into a certain number of shares of stock at the option of the bondholder.

- The **conversion ratio** is the number of shares the holder receives from conversion for each bond. **Conversion value** is calculated as:

$$\text{conversion value} = \text{market price of stock} \times \text{conversion ratio}$$

- The **straight value**, or investment value, of a convertible bond is the value of the bond if it were not convertible—the present value of the bond's cash flows discounted at the required return on a comparable option-free issue.
- The **minimum value** of a convertible bond must be the greater of its conversion value or its straight value.
- The **market conversion price** is the price effectively paid for the stock by buying the bond and converting:

$$\text{market conversion price} = \frac{\text{market price of convertible}}{\text{conversion ratio}}$$

Most convertible bonds are callable, giving the issuer the right to call the issue prior to maturity. Incorporating this feature into the valuation of a convertible bond results in the following expression:

$$\begin{aligned}\text{callable convertible bond value} &= \text{straight value of bond} \\ &\quad + \text{value of the call option on the stock} \\ &\quad - \text{value of the call option on the bond}\end{aligned}$$

The valuation of a callable convertible bond involves the valuation of the call feature, which is a function of interest rate volatility and the economic conditions that can trigger the call feature. The Black-Scholes option pricing model *cannot* be used in this situation.

For a callable convertible bond:

- An increase in stock price volatility will increase the value of the call on the stock and increase the value of the callable convertible bond.
- An increase in interest rate volatility will increase the value of the call on the bond and reduce the value of the callable convertible bond.

Buying convertible bonds in lieu of stocks limits downside risk. The price floor set by the straight bond value causes this downside protection. The cost of the downside protection is reduced upside potential due to the conversion premium. In addition, the coupons on convertibles are smaller than on otherwise comparable straight bonds.

Mortgage-Backed Sector of the Bond Market

Cross-Reference to CFA Institute Assigned Topic Review #45

A **mortgage-backed security** (MBS) is a bond whose cash flows are derived from a pool of mortgage loans (mortgage loans are loans used to finance the purchase of real estate). Most of the mortgage loans used as collateral for MBS are fixed-rate, fully amortizing loans. This means the payments from the mortgages don't change as interest rates change, and the payments include both principal and interest.

Prepayment Risk

The difficult feature of MBS valuation is that the underlying mortgages are subject to prepayment. This means the borrowers can prepay all or part of the principal value at any time. To a large extent, this **prepayment risk** is associated with interest rates (as interest rates fall, the borrowers tend to refinance their mortgage loans at lower rates, causing high prepayments on mortgages in the existing MBS pool).

The simplest type of MBS is a **passthrough security**. With a mortgage passthrough, all payments from the underlying mortgages (both principal and interest) are passed along to the security holders on a *pro rata* basis. The problem with valuing a passthrough is that there is great uncertainty about what the cash flow pattern will be because of prepayment risk. Be familiar with the following terms associated with prepayment rates:

- The **conditional prepayment rate** (CPR) is the annual rate at which a mortgage pool is expected to be prepaid. This is a generic term for the rate of prepayment; there is no specific schedule.
- The **Public Securities Association** (PSA) **prepayment benchmark** is a specific assumption about the prepayment rate of a mortgage pool. The PSA assumes the mortgage pool monthly prepayments start at a 0.2% annual rate and increase by 0.2% each month for the first 30 months of the life of the pool (after month 30, the prepayment rate is constant at 6%).
- **Single monthly mortality** (SMM) **rate**. The PSA is stated in annual terms (e.g., the pool will prepay in month 1 at a 0.2% annual rate). You can convert the annual rate to a monthly percentage with the following formula: $SMM = 1 - (1 - CPR)^{1/12}$.

The speed of prepayment will be influenced by three factors:

1. **Prevailing mortgage rates** affect prepayments in at least two ways:
    - *Spread between the current mortgage rate and the original mortgage rate.* If a homeowner is holding a high interest rate mortgage and current mortgage rates fall, the incentive to refinance is large.

- *Path of mortgage rates.* The path that mortgage rates follow on their way to the current level will affect prepayments today. The tendency for prepayments to be less the second time a lower rate is reached (when rates fall, rise, and fall again) is called refinancing burnout.

2. **Housing turnover** increases as rates fall and housing becomes more affordable. Housing turnover is also higher when economic growth is higher.
3. Two particular **characteristics of the underlying mortgages** also affect the level of prepayments: seasoning (i.e., the age of the loan) and property location. Prepayments are low for new mortgages but increase as the loan seasons (the PSA benchmark reflects this idea). Local economics also influence prepayments, which tend to be faster in some parts of the country and slower in others.

Contraction and Extension Risk

Contraction risk refers to the shortening of the expected life of the mortgage pool due to falling interest rates and higher prepayment rates.

Extension risk is associated with interest rate increases and falling prepayment rates. Bond prices typically fall when interest rates rise. With passthroughs, the accompanying decrease in prepayments compounds this price decline, because the timing of the passthrough cash flows is extended further than originally expected (i.e., the average life of the bond is extended).

In summary:

- Contraction risk occurs as mortgage rates fall, prepayment rates increase, and the average life of the passthrough security decreases.
- Extension risk occurs as mortgage rates rise, prepayment rates slow, and the average life of the passthrough security increases.

Collateralized Mortgage Obligations (CMOs)

CMOs are securities issued against passthrough securities (securities secured by other securities) for which the cash flows have been reallocated to different bond classes called *tranches*, each having a different claim against the cash flows of the mortgage passthroughs or pool from which they were derived. Each CMO tranche represents a different mixture of contraction and extension risk. Hence, CMO securities can be more closely matched to the unique asset/liability needs of institutional investors and investment managers.

You should understand the structure and prepayment risk of these types of CMO tranches:

- *Sequential-pay tranches*. In sequential-pay tranches, each class of bond is retired sequentially. Contraction and extension risk still exist with this structure, but they have been redistributed to some extent between the tranches. The short tranche, which matures first, offers investors relatively more protection against extension risk. The other tranches provide relatively more protection against contraction risk.
- *Accrual bonds*. For many sequential-pay CMO structures, the last tranche to be paid principal also does not receive current interest until the other tranches have been paid off. This tranche is called the *Z-tranche* or *accrual tranche*, and the securities that represent a claim against its cash flows are called Z-bonds or accrual bonds. The interest that would ordinarily be paid to the accrual tranche is applied against the outstanding principal of the other tranches, in sequence. The accrual bond absorbs most of the extension risk in a sequential-pay structure.
- *Planned amortization class (PAC) tranches*. These are tranches that are amortized based on a sinking fund schedule that is established within a range of prepayment speeds called the *initial PAC collar* or *initial PAC bond*. There are two principal repayment schedules associated with a PAC bond, one for the lower prepayment rate and one for the upper rate of the initial PAC collar. PAC tranches have lower contraction and extension risk than their support tranches.
- *Support tranches*. Support tranches are included in a structure with PAC tranches, specifically to provide prepayment protection for the PAC tranches. There is an inverse relationship between the prepayment risk of PAC tranches and the prepayment risk associated with the support tranches. In other words, the certainty of PAC bond cash flow comes at the expense of increased risk to the support tranches.
- *Stripped mortgage-backed securities (STRIPS)*. A strip is a security that receives only the interest payments (an IO strip) or only the principal payments (a PO strip) from the underlying pool.
    - The investment performance of a PO is extremely sensitive to prepayment rates. Higher prepayment rates result in a faster-than-expected return of principal and, thus, a higher yield. PO prices increase when interest rates fall.
    - The IO price is positively related to mortgage rates at low current rates. When market rates decline below the average mortgage rate in the pool, prepayment rates increase and the principal amount falls. Interest payments to the IO decrease because they are based on the outstanding principal on the underlying pool. The diminished cash flow usually causes the IO price to decline, despite the fact the cash flows are now being discounted at a lower rate.
    - Both IOs and POs exhibit greater *price volatility* than the passthrough from which they were derived.

Commercial MBS

Commercial mortgage-backed securities (CMBS) are collateralized by a pool of commercial mortgage loans on income-producing properties, such as warehouses, office buildings, or apartments.

There are two important differences between residential MBS and CMBS:

1. Residential MBS loans are repaid by homeowners; CMBS loans are repaid by real estate investors who, in turn, rely on tenants and customers to provide the cash flow to repay the mortgage loan.
2. CMBS mortgages are structured as *non-recourse* loans, meaning the lender can only look to the collateral as means to repay the loan. The residential mortgage lender can go back to the borrower personally in an attempt to repay a delinquent mortgage loan.

For these reasons, the analysis of CMBS securities focuses on the credit risk of the property and not the borrower. CMBS structures focus on two key ratios to assess credit risk:

$$\text{debt-to-service coverage ratio} = \frac{\text{net operating income}}{\text{debt service}}$$

$$\text{loan-to-value ratio} = \frac{\text{current mortgage amount}}{\text{current appraised value}}$$

Loan-level call protection is created by a prepayment lockout, defeasance, prepayment penalty points, and yield maintenance charges. *CMBS-level call protection* is created by segregating pools into credit tranches.

Asset-Backed Sector of the Bond Market

Cross-Reference to CFA Institute Assigned Topic Review #46

Asset-backed securities (ABS) are backed by pools of loans or receivables other than primary mortgages. Some ABS are backed by amortizing loans (with scheduled principal payments), and others are backed by non-amortizing loans (with no scheduled principal payments).

Basic Features of a Securitization Transaction

The key parties to a securitization transaction are:

- The seller, who originates the loans and sells them to the issuer/trust.
- The issuer/trust, who buys the loans from the seller and issues the ABS.
- The servicer, who services the original loans.

See Figure 4 for an example of Fred Motor Company, which wants to remove $1 billion in auto loans from its balance sheet.

Figure 5: Structure of Fred Motor Company Asset Securitization

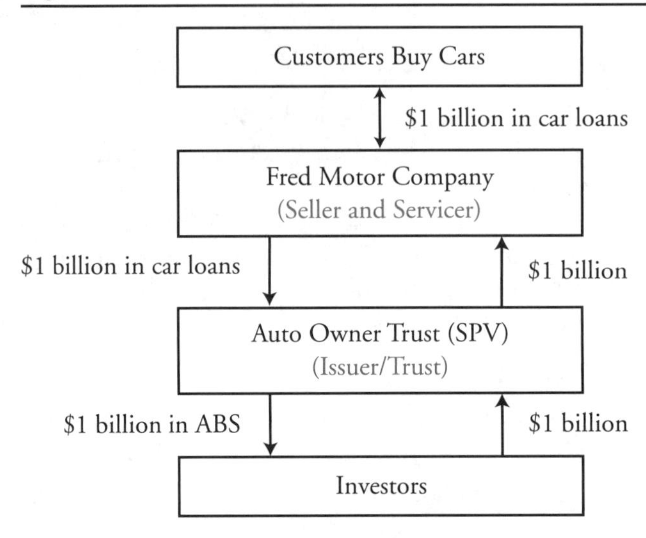

Prepayments and Credit Tranching

- *Prepayment tranching or time tranching:* ABS structures are divided into different tranches to distribute the prepayment risk to various investors using, for example, sequential-pay or PAC structures.
- *Credit tranching:* In a senior-subordinated structure, the subordinated bonds absorb losses first up to their par value, after which losses are absorbed by the senior bonds. The result is to transfer some of the credit risk from the senior bonds to the subordinated bonds.

Credit Enhancements

Most ABS require credit enhancement. Credit enhancement comes in two forms:

1. *External credit enhancements* are financial guarantees from third parties that support the performance of the bond. External credit enhancements include *corporate guarantees*, *letters of credit*, and *bond insurance*. The problem with third-party guarantees is the "weak link" philosophy adopted by rating agencies: the credit quality of an issue cannot be higher than the credit rating of the third-party guarantor.

2. *Internal credit enhancements* include reserve funds, overcollateralization, and structures that contain senior and subordinated debt. Internal credit enhancements do not rely on a third-party guarantee.

Types of ABS

There are several classes of assets that are used to create ABS. The most common are as follows:

- **Closed-end home equity loans** (HELs) are secondary mortgages structured just like a standard fixed-rate, fully amortizing mortgage. The pattern of prepayments from HELs differs from MBS prepayment patterns primarily because of differences in the credit traits of the borrowers. Therefore, analysts must consider the credit of the borrowers when analyzing HEL-backed securities. HEL floaters have a variable coupon rate cap called the available funds cap. HEL structures frequently include non-accelerating senior tranches and planned amortization class (PAC) tranches.
- **Manufactured housing ABS** are backed by loans for manufactured homes. Prepayments for manufactured ABS are relatively stable because the underlying loans are not as sensitive to refinancing because:
    - Small loan balances reduce the extent of savings resulting from refinancing.
    - Initial depreciation of mobile homes may be such that the loan principal exceeds the asset value.
    - Borrowers often have relatively low credit ratings, making it difficult to refinance.
- **Auto loan-backed securities** are backed by loans for automobiles. Auto loans have 36- to 72-month maturities and are issued by the financial subsidiaries of auto manufacturers, commercial banks, credit unions, et cetera. Prepayments for auto loan-backed securities are caused by sales and trade-ins, the repossession/resale prices, insurance payoffs due to thefts and accidents, borrower payoffs, and refinancing. Refinancing is of minor importance, since many auto loans are frequently below market rates due to sales promotions.
- **Student loan ABS** are most often securitized by loans made under the U.S. government's FFELP. Qualifying FFELP loans carry a U.S. government guarantee. Prepayments may occur because of defaults (inflows from the government guarantee process) or loan consolidation.
- **SBA loan-backed securities** are backed by pools of SBA loans with similar terms and features. Most SBA loans are variable-rate loans, reset quarterly or monthly, and based on the prime rate.

- **Credit-card receivables ABS** are backed by pools of receivables owed by banks, retailers, travel and entertainment companies, and other credit card issuers. The cash flow to a pool of credit card receivables includes finance charges, annual fees, and principal repayments. Credit cards have periodic payment schedules, but since their balances are revolving, the principal is not amortized. Because of this characteristic, interest on credit card ABS is paid periodically, but no principal is paid to the ABS holders during the lockout period, which may last from 18 months to 10 years.

Collateralized Debt Obligations

Collateralized debt obligations (CDOs) are collateralized by a pool of debt obligations comprised of one or more of the following assets: corporate bonds, MBS and ABS, bond issues in emerging markets, corporate loans advanced by commercial banks, and special situations and distressed debt.

The securities that back a cash CDO are cash market debt securities, such as corporate bonds, previously described. Cash CDOs can be arbitrage-driven, in which the motivation is to generate an arbitrage return on the spread between return on the collateral and the funding costs, or balance sheet-driven, in which the motivation is to remove assets (and the associated funding) from the balance sheet.

In a *synthetic CDO*, the bondholders take on the economic risks of the underlying assets but do not take legal ownership of them. This is accomplished by linking certain contingent payments to a reference asset (e.g., a bond index). There are three advantages to a synthetic CDO versus a cash CDO:

1. The senior section doesn't require funding.
2. The ramp-up period is shorter.
3. It's cheaper to acquire an exposure to the reference asset through a credit default swap instead of buying the asset directly.

Valuing Mortgage-Backed and Asset-Backed Securities

Cross-Reference to CFA Institute Assigned Topic Review #47

For exposition purposes, we focus on valuing MBS, but keep in mind that most of these concepts also apply directly to ABS valuation.

Spread Measures Related to MBS and ABS

- The *cash flow yield* is the discount rate that makes the price of a mortgage-backed security (MBS) or asset-backed security (ABS) equal to the present value of its cash flows. The challenge in applying this concept is that the cash flows from the MBS or ABS are uncertain because we don't know what future prepayment rates will be. The cash flow yield has three major deficiencies regarding assumptions: (1) we assume the cash flows will be reinvested at the cash flow yield prevailing when the MBS or ABS is priced (referred to as reinvestment risk in other areas of the CFA curriculum); (2) we assume the MBS or ABS will be held until maturity—price risk occurs if the security is sold prior to maturity; and (3) we assume the cash flows will be realized.

- The *nominal spread* is the difference between the cash flow yield (think IRR) on an MBS and the yield on a Treasury security with a maturity equal to the average life of the MBS. The limitation of using the nominal spread to analyze MBS is that we don't know how much of the nominal spread reflects the significant prepayment risk associated with MBS.
- The *zero-volatility spread* (Z-spread) is the spread that must be added to Treasury spot rates in order to make the calculated price of the bond equal to the market price. The limitation of the Z-spread is that it considers only one interest rate path (the current spot rate curve).
- The *option-adjusted spread* (OAS) is calculated as the spread that must be added to every nodal interest rate on every interest rate path on an interest rate tree in order to make the model price of the bond equal to the market price. It can be interpreted as the spread for the MBS's liquidity and default risk, with the effect of the option on yields removed.

Path Dependency

Since prepayments and MBS cash flows depend not only on interest rates but also on the path rates have taken to get there, Monte Carlo simulation, instead of the binomial model, must be used to value these securities. There are two sources of path dependency:

1. If mortgage rates trend downward over a period of time, prepayment rates will increase at the beginning of the trend as homeowners refinance their mortgages; but prepayments will slow as the trend continues, because many of the homeowners that can refinance will have already done so. This prepayment pattern is called **prepayment burnout**, and it applies to MBS and other types of passthrough security cash flows.
2. The cash flows a particular tranche receives in any one month depend on the outstanding principal balances of the other tranches in the structure, which in turn depend on the prepayment history and the interest rate path.

OAS Analysis

We can interpret the OAS as the MBS spread after the yield effect of the prepayment option is taken into account. The implied cost of the embedded option can be expressed as:

option cost = zero-volatility spread – option-adjusted spread

A greater OAS for one security compared to another of similar credit risk, liquidity risk, and maturity. Investors want to buy the bond with the bigger OAS.

The interpretation of the OAS depends on the security's credit risk, liquidity risk, and modeling risk relative to the benchmark.

- If we use Treasury securities as the benchmark, the OAS on a Ginnie Mae passthrough (which carries the full faith and credit of the U.S. government) reflects liquidity risk and modeling risk. The CMOs themselves issued by Ginnie Mae (which are backed by the passthroughs) carry additional modeling risk. Also, support tranches carry more liquidity risk and modeling risk than PAC I tranches, so they should have a higher OAS.
- Freddie Mac and Fannie Mae securities, which are government-sponsored agencies, also have some small degree of credit risk, so the OAS of these securities reflects credit risk, liquidity risk, and modeling risk.
- The OAS for non-agency MBS and real-estate backed ABS reflects credit risk, additional liquidity risk to agency-backed MBS, and modeling risk.

Figure 6: Interpretation of OAS Using Treasury Securities as a Benchmark

	Does the OAS Using a Treasury Benchmark Reflect:		
Security	*Credit Risk?*	*Liquidity Risk?*	*Modeling Risk?*
Ginnie Mae passthroughs	No	Yes	Yes
Ginnie Mae CMOs	No	Yes. Support tranches have more than PAC I.	Yes. CMOs have more than passthroughs. CMO support tranches have more than PAC I.
Freddie Mac / Fannie Mae passthroughs	Yes, but small.	Yes	Yes
Freddie Mac / Fannie Mae CMOs	Yes, but small.	Yes. CMO support tranches have more than PAC I.	Yes. CMOs have more than passthroughs. CMO support tranches have more than PAC I.
Non-agency MBS and real estate-backed ABS	Yes	Yes, more than agency issues.	Yes

We can identify rich and cheap securities by comparing the OAS and option costs of the various tranches in a CMO deal. Securities with longer effective durations have larger OAS and option costs because of their higher interest rate exposure. Therefore, for a given Z-spread and effective duration:

- *Cheap* securities (we should buy these) will have high OAS and low option costs.
- *Rich* securities (we should sell these) will have low OAS and high option costs.

Spread Analysis

The decision to use nominal spread, zero-volatility spread, or OAS to assess the value of any asset depends on the characteristics of the asset being evaluated. Figure 6 outlines when each spread measure should be used.

Figure 7: Appropriate Spread Measures for Fixed Income Securities

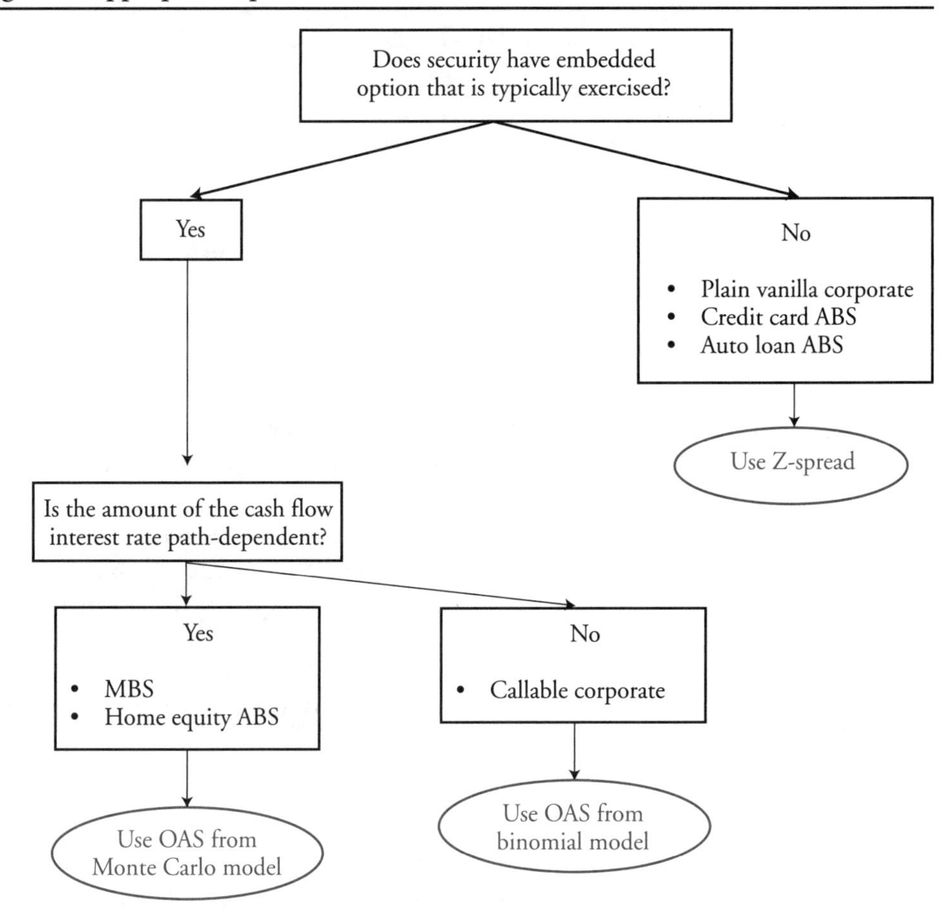

Derivatives

Study Sessions 16 & 17

Topic Weight on Exam	5–15%
SchweserNotes™ Reference	Book 5, Pages 8–148

Forward Markets and Contracts

Cross-Reference to CFA Institute Assigned Topic Review #48

A clear understanding of the sources and timing of forward contract settlement payments will enable you to be successful on this portion of the exam without depending on pure memorization of these complex formulas.

Pricing vs. Valuation of Forward Contracts

- The *price* of a forward contract is the price specified in the contract at which the long and short sides have agreed to trade the underlying asset when the contract expires.
- The *value* of a forward contract to each side is the amount of money the counterparty would be willing to pay (or receive) to terminate the contract. It's a zero-sum game, so the value of the long position is equal to the negative of the value of the short position.
- The *no-arbitrage* price of the forward contract (with a maturity of *T* years) is the price at which the value of the long side and the value of the short side are both equal to zero.

$$FP = S_0 \times (1 + R_f)^T$$

The value of the long position in a forward contract at initiation, during the contract life, and at maturity are shown in Figure 1.

Figure 1: Forward Value of Long Position at Initiation, During the Contract Life, and at Expiration

Time	*Forward Contract Valuation (Long Position)*
At initiation	Zero, because the contract is priced to prevent arbitrage
During the life of the contract	$S_t - \left[\dfrac{FP}{(1+R_f)^{T-t}}\right]$
At expiration	$S_T - FP$

The value of the short position at any point in time is the negative of the long position.

Forward Contract on a Stock

A stock, a stock portfolio, or an equity index may have expected dividend payments over the life of the contract. In order to price such a contract, we must either adjust the spot price for the present value of the expected dividends (PVD) or adjust the forward price for the future value of the dividends (FVD):

$$FP(\text{on a stock}) = (S_0 - PVD) \times (1+R_f)^T = \left[S_0 \times (1+R_f)^T\right] - FVD$$

To calculate the *value* of the long position in a forward contract on a dividend-paying stock, we make the adjustment for the present value of the remaining expected discrete dividends at time *t* (PVD_t) to get:

$$V_t(\text{long position on a stock}) = (S_t - PVD_t) - \left(\frac{FP}{(1+R_f)^{T-t}}\right)$$

Forward Contract on Equity Index

The dividends on an equity index are approximately continuous, so to price and value a forward contract on an equity index, use the same basic formulas with continuous compounding at the continuously compounded risk-free rate of R_f^c and assume a continuous dividend yield of δ^c.

$$FP(\text{on equity index}) = S_0 \times e^{\left(R_f^c - \delta^c\right) \times T}$$

$$V_t(\text{long position on equity index}) = \left(\frac{S_t}{e^{\delta^c \times (T-t)}}\right) - \left(\frac{FP}{e^{R_f^c \times (T-t)}}\right)$$

Forwards on Fixed Income Securities

To calculate the no-arbitrage forward price and value on a coupon-paying bond, substitute the present value of the expected coupon payments (PVC) *over the life of the contract* for the present value of the expected dividends to get:

$$\text{FP(on fixed income security)} = (S_0 - \text{PVC}) \times (1 + R_f)^T$$

$$V_t\text{(long position on fixed income security)} = (S_t - \text{PVC}_t) - \left(\frac{\text{FP}}{(1 + R_f)^{T-t}}\right)$$

Forward Rate Agreements (FRAs)

Basics of FRAs:

- The long position in an FRA is the party that would borrow the money (long the loan with the contract price being the interest rate on the loan).
- If LIBOR at expiration is above the rate specified in the forward agreement, the long position in the contract can be viewed as the right to borrow at below market rates, and the long will receive a payment.
- If rates at the expiration date are below the then-current market rates, the short will receive a cash payment from the long. (The right to lend at *above* market rates would have a positive value.)
- The notation for FRAs is unique. For example, a 2×3 FRA is a contract that expires in two months (60 days), and the underlying loan is settled in three months (90 days). The underlying rate is 1-month (30-day) LIBOR on a 30-day loan in 60 days. A timeline for a 2×3 FRA is shown in Figure 2.

Figure 2: Illustration of a 2×3 FRA

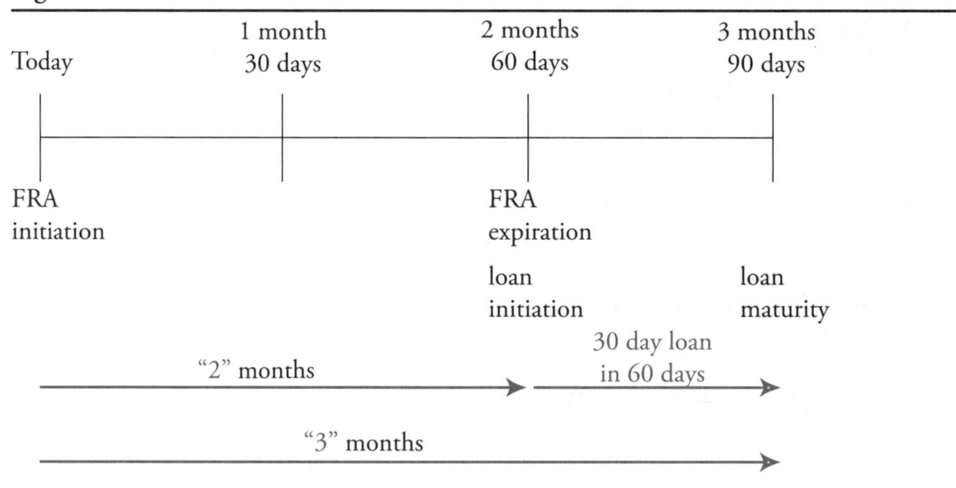

Pricing an FRA

The "price" of the FRA is actually the forward interest rate implied by the spot rates consistent with the FRA. For example, the "price" of the 2×3 FRA is the 30-day forward rate in 60 days implied by the 60- and 90-day spot rates.

Valuing an FRA

The value of an FRA to the long or short position comes from the interest savings on a loan to be made at the settlement date. This value is to be received at the end of the loan, so the value of an FRA after initiation is the present value of these savings. Remember, if the rate in the future is less than the FRA rate, the long is "obligated to borrow" at above-market rates and will have to make a payment to the short. If the rate is greater than the FRA rate, the long will receive a payment from the short.

Let's outline the general steps for valuing a 2×3 FRA (a 30-day loan in 60 days) 40 days after initiation (which means there are 20 days remaining until the FRA expires).

Step 1: Calculate the implied *30-day forward rate* at the settlement date, 20 days from now, using the current 20-day spot rate and the current 50-day spot rate.

Step 2: Calculate the value of the FRA at maturity as the notional principal times the difference between the forward rate from Step 1 and the original FRA "price." Make sure to convert from an annual rate to a 30-day rate. If the current forward rate is greater than the original FRA price, the long position has positive value. If the current forward rate is less than the original FRA price, the short position has positive value.

Step 3: Calculate the value of the FRA today by discounting the value at maturity from Step 2 at the 50-day spot rate.

Currency Forwards

The pricing and valuation of a currency forward contract is straightforward. The calculation of the currency forward rate is an application of covered interest parity from the topic review of international parity relations in Study Session 4.

Covered interest rate parity gives us the no-arbitrage forward price of a unit of foreign currency in terms of the home currency (DC/FC) for a currency forward contract:

$$F_T = (\text{currency forward contract}) = S_0 \times e^{\left(R^c_{DC} - R^c_{FC}\right) \times T}$$

F and *S* are quoted in domestic currency units per one unit of foreign currency.

At any time prior to maturity, the value of a currency forward contract to the long will depend on the spot rate at time *t* and S_t:

$$V_t(\text{currency forward contract}) = \left[\frac{S_t}{(1 + R_{FC})^{T-t}}\right] - \left[\frac{F_t}{(1+R_{DC})^{T-t}}\right]$$

Futures Markets and Contracts

Cross-Reference to CFA Institute Assigned Topic Review #49

Pricing Futures Contracts

The no-arbitrage price of a futures contract on an asset with no storage costs or cash flows is approximately the same as that of a forward contract on the asset:

$$FP = S_0 \times (1 + R_f)^T$$

However, the mark-to-market feature of futures contracts will cause futures and forward prices to be slightly different.

Figure 3: Prices of Futures vs. Forward Contracts

If the correlation between the underlying asset value and interest rates is...	*Investors will...*
Positive	Prefer to go long in a **futures contract** and the futures price will be greater than the price of an otherwise comparable forward contract
Zero	Have no preference
Negative	Prefer to go long in a **forward contract** and the forward price will be greater than the price of an otherwise comparable futures contract

Valuing Futures Contracts

Futures contracts are marked-to-market daily, so the value to both sides of the contract is zero at the end of the trading day. Therefore, the contract only has value during the trading day:

$$\text{futures contract value} = \text{current futures price} - \text{futures price at last mark-to-market}$$

Futures Arbitrage

If the futures contract is overpriced (actual futures market price is greater than the no-arbitrage price), *cash-and-carry arbitrage* will generate a riskless profit:

- At the initiation of the contract:
  1. Borrow money for the term of the contract at the risk-free rate.
  2. Buy the underlying asset at the spot price.
  3. Sell a futures contract at the current futures price.

- At contract expiration:
  4. Deliver the asset and receive the futures contract price.
  5. Repay the loan plus interest.

If the futures contract is underpriced (futures market price is less than the no-arbitrage price), *reverse cash-and-carry arbitrage* will earn an arbitrage profit:

- At the initiation of the contract:
  1. Sell the asset short.
  2. Lend the short sale proceeds at the risk-free rate.
  3. Buy the futures contract at market price.

- At contract expiration:
  4. Collect loan proceeds.
  5. Take delivery of the asset for the futures price and cover the short sale commitment.

Monetary and Non-Monetary Benefits and Costs of Holding the Underlying Asset

Future prices are affected by the monetary costs and benefits (i.e., net costs, or NC) of holding the underlying asset. Storage and insurance are costs, while any cash flows from the asset are a benefit:

$$FP = S_0 \times (1 + R_f)^T + FV(NC)$$

There can also be *non-monetary benefits* (i.e., net benefits, or NB) from holding assets and having the use of them. This non-monetary return is termed a convenience yield. In that case, the no-arbitrage futures price is:

$$FP = S_0 \times (1 + R_f)^T - FV(NB)$$

Futures Prices as Predictors of Future Asset Prices

One issue in futures pricing is whether the futures price is equal to the expected future price of the asset. Any difference is due to risk (i.e., the uncertainty about the future asset price). If futures buyers are taking risk from asset owners and require a premium for doing so, the futures price will be less than the expected spot price, a situation described as *normal backwardation.*

It is also possible that futures buyers are seeking to reduce the asset price risk they currently have because of their need to purchase the asset in the future. In this case, there may be no risk premium, or even a negative premium, if futures buyers are willing to pay a higher price because of the risk reduction benefits to them of a long futures position. If this results in futures prices greater than expected future spot prices, the situation is referred to as *normal contango.* Note that normal backwardation and normal contango are different from backwardation and contango.

- **Backwardation.** Futures price is less than spot price.
- **Contango.** Futures price is greater than spot price.
- **Normal backwardation**. Futures price is less than *expected* spot price.
- **Normal contango**. Futures price is greater than *expected* spot price.

Eurodollar Contract Pricing Difficulty

Eurodollar futures are priced as a discount yield, and LIBOR-based deposits are priced as an add-on yield. The result is that the deposit value is not perfectly hedged by the Eurodollar contract, so Eurodollar futures can't be priced using the standard no-arbitrage framework.

Pricing Treasury Bond, Equity Index, and Currency Futures

The price of a Treasury **bond future** that settles at time = T is calculated as the future value of the bond minus the future value of the bonds cash flows over the life of the futures contract, adjusted by the conversion factor (CF) of the cheapest-to-deliver (CTD) bond under the terms of the futures contract.

$$\text{FP(T-bond)} = \frac{\text{PV of CTD bond } [(1+R_f(T))]^T - FV_T \text{ (interest cash flows 0,T)}}{\text{CF(CTD bond)}}$$

In order to price equity or *stock index future* of period T, we need to adjust for the dividend yield, either as a discrete annual rate (δ) or a continuously compounded rate (δ^C) to get:

$$FP(Index) = \frac{S_0}{(1+\delta)^T}(1+R)^T \text{ or in continuous time,}$$
$$FP(Index) = S_0 e^{(R^C - \delta^C)T}$$

In order to price a currency future, we must take account of the difference in yield between the futures contract currency return (R) and the underlying asset currency return ($R_{foreign}$):

$$FP(Index) = \frac{S_0}{(1+R_{foreign})^T}(1+R)^T \text{ or in continuous time,}$$
$$FP(Index) = S_0 e^{(R^C - R^C_{foreign})T}$$

Option Markets and Contracts

Cross-Reference to CFA Institute Assigned Topic Review #50

Put-Call Parity for European Options

Put-call parity must hold by arbitrage:

$$C_0 + \left[\frac{X}{(1+R_f)^T}\right] = P_0 + S_0$$

or

call + riskless discount bond = put + stock

or

fiduciary call = protective put

Use put-call parity to create *synthetic instruments*. Interpret "+" as a long position and "–" as a short position:

synthetic call = put + stock – riskless discount bond
synthetic put = call – stock + riskless discount bond
synthetic stock = call – put + riskless discount bond
synthetic riskless discount bond = put + stock – call

Violations of put-call parity are exploited by buying the underpriced component and shorting the overpriced component:

- If fiduciary call > protective put, sell fiduciary call, buy protective put.
- If fiduciary call < protective put, buy fiduciary call, sell protective put.

The Binomial Option Pricing Model (OPM)

The binomial process generates stock price paths, just as the binomial interest rate model generates interest rate paths. However, whereas the probabilities of an up or down movement are the same (equal 0.5) in an interest rate tree, these so-called pseudo probabilities are usually not equal (but still must sum to 1.0) in a stock price tree.

We can calculate the value of an option on the stock by:

- Calculating the payoff of the option at maturity in both the up-move and down-move states.
- Calculating the expected value of the option in one year as the probability-weighted average of the payoffs in each state.
- Discounting the expected value back to today at the risk-free rate.

Let's calculate the *value* today of a 1-period call option on a stock with an exercise price of \$30. Assume the risk-free rate is 7%, the current value of the stock is \$30, and the size of an up-move (U) is 1.333, as shown in Figure 4.

Figure 4: 1-Period Binomial Tree

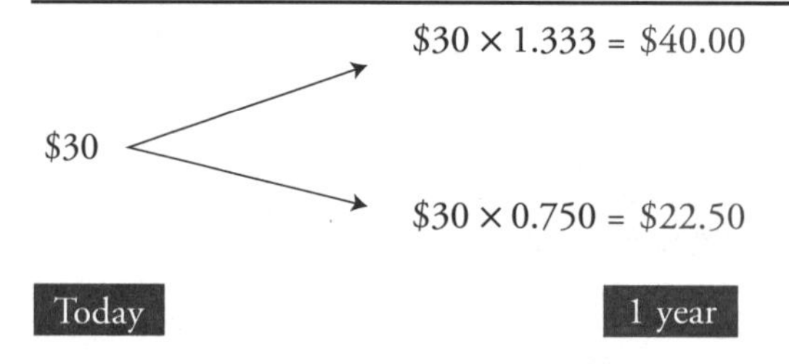

The size of the downward movement (D) factor is:

$$D = \frac{1}{U} = \frac{1}{1.333} = 0.75$$

The risk-neutral probability of an upward movement is:

$$\pi_U = \frac{1 + R_f - D}{U - D} = \frac{1.07 - 0.75}{1.333 - 0.75} = 0.55$$

The risk-neutral probability of a downward movement is then:

$$\pi_D = 1 - \pi_U = 1 - 0.55 = 0.45$$

The binomial tree for the stock and the option is shown in Figure 5.

Figure 5: 1-Period Call Option With X = $30

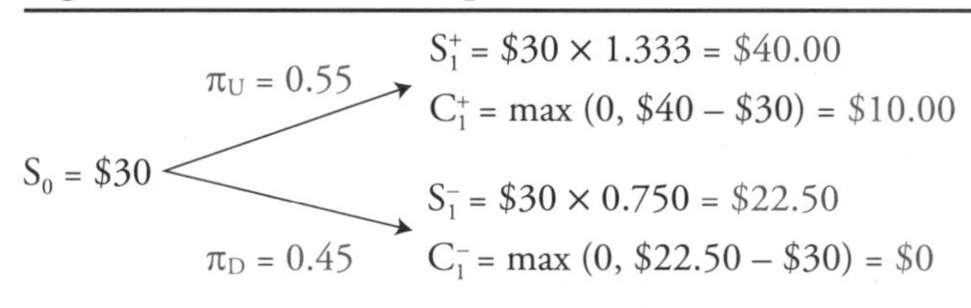

The call option is in-the-money in the "up" state, so its terminal value is $10. It is out-of-the-money in the "down" state, so its terminal value is zero.

The expected value of the option in one year is:

$$(\$10 \times 0.55) + (\$0 \times 0.45) = \$5.50$$

The present value of the call option's expected value today is:

$$c = \frac{\$5.50}{1.07} = \$5.14$$

Options on Fixed Income Securities

To price options on bonds, we need a binomial interest rate tree that shows possible future 1-period interest rates. The risk-free rate is not constant, however. Since the tree gives us a series of 1-period rates, we need to discount the payments by one or more of these rates, depending on how many periods the payoff is out (to the right) on the tree.

There are three basic steps to valuing an option on a fixed-income instrument using a binomial tree:

Step 1: Price the bond at each node using the projected interest rates.

Step 2: Establish the intrinsic value of the option at each node at the maturity of the option.
Step 3: Bring the terminal option values determined in Step 2 back to today.

We assume that the probability of an up- and down-move in the interest rate tree is always 50%.

Options on Interest Rates: Caps and Floors

Steps in *valuing a 2-year cap or floor:*

Step 1: Calculate the expiration value of the 2-year caplet or floorlet at each node at the end of year 2 using the appropriate formula:

$$\text{expiration value of caplet} = \frac{\max\left[0, (\text{1-yr. rate} - \text{cap rate}) \times \text{notional prin.}\right]}{1 + \text{1-yr. rate}}$$

$$\text{expiration value of floorlet} = \frac{\max\left[0, (\text{floor rate} - \text{1-yr. rate}) \times \text{notional prin.}\right]}{1 + \text{1-yr. rate}}$$

Step 2: Bring the terminal caplet or floorlet values from Step 1 back to today. The probabilities of up- and down-moves are 50%.
Step 3: Repeat Steps 1 and 2 for the 1-year caplet or floorlet.
Step 4: Calculate the value of the interest rate cap as the sum of values of individual caplets, or the value of the interest rate floor as the sum of values of individual floorlets.

The Black-Scholes-Merton Option Pricing Model Assumptions and Limitations

The *assumptions* underlying the Black-Scholes-Merton (BSM) model are:

- The price of the underlying asset follows a lognormal distribution.
- The (continuous) risk-free rate is constant and known.
- The volatility of the underlying asset is constant and known.
- Markets are frictionless.
- The underlying asset generates no cash flows.
- The options are European.

Because of the limitations of these assumptions, the BSM model is *not appropriate*:

- For valuing interest rate options and options on bond prices because the assumption of a constant and known risk-free rate is violated.
- When the assumption of a constant and known volatility of underlying asset returns is violated.

- In cases where taxes and transactions costs are significant.
- For pricing American-style options.

Inputs to the Black-Scholes-Merton Model

There are five inputs to the BSM model: asset price, exercise price, asset price volatility, time to expiration, and the risk-free rate. The effects of changes in each input (in isolation, holding all else constant) on the value of European call and put options (on assets with no cash flows) are outlined in Figure 6.

Figure 6: BSM Sensitivities

Sensitivity Factor ("Greek")	*Input*	*Calls*	*Puts*
Delta	Asset price (S)	Positively related delta > 0	Negatively related delta < 0
Vega	Volatility (σ)	Positively related vega > 0	Positively related vega > 0
Rho	Risk-free rate (r)	Positively related rho > 0	Negatively related rho < 0
Theta	Time to expiration (T)	Value → \$0 as call → maturity theta < 0	Value usually → 0 as put → maturity theta < 0*
	Exercise price (X)	Negatively related	Positively related

* There is an exception to the general rule that European put option thetas are negative. The put value may increase as the option approaches maturity if the option is deep in the money and close to maturity.

Delta

An option's *delta* estimates the change in the value of the option for a 1-unit change in the value of the underlying stock.

$$\text{delta}_{\text{call}} = \frac{\text{change in call price}}{\text{change in stock price}}$$

For small changes in stock price, a call option's delta is $N(d_1)$ from the BSM; the comparable put option's delta is $N(d_1) - 1$. The following relationships are approximations:

$$\text{change in call price} \approx N(d_1) \times \text{change in stock price}$$

$$\text{change in put price} \approx [N(d_1) - 1] \times \text{change in stock price}$$

Figure 7: Delta: Key Points to Remember

Option	*Range*	*Far Out-of-the-Money*	*Far In-the-Money*	*As Stock Price Increases*
Call	0 to 1	Close to 0	Close to 1	Increases from 0 to 1
Put	–1 to 0	Close to 0	Close to –1	Increases from –1 to 0

Delta-Neutral Hedging

A *delta-neutral portfolio* is a combination of short call options with the underlying stock so that the value of the portfolio doesn't change when the value of the stock changes. The number of call options to sell to create the delta-neutral hedge is as follows:

$$\text{number of call options needed to delta hedge} = \frac{\text{number of shares hedged}}{\text{delta of call option}}$$

The delta-neutral position only holds for very small changes in the value of the underlying stock. Hence, the delta-neutral portfolio must be continuously rebalanced to maintain the hedge. This is called a dynamic hedge.

Gamma

Gamma measures the rate of change in delta as the underlying stock price changes. Gamma is largest when the option is at-the-money, so delta is very sensitive to changes in the underlying stock price when the option is at-the-money.

Gamma can be viewed as a measure of how poorly a dynamic hedge will perform when it is not rebalanced in response to a change in the asset price. Hedges with at-the-money options will have higher gammas, and consequently small changes in stock price will lead to large changes in delta and frequent rebalancing.

Options on Forwards and Futures

Put-call parity for options on forwards and futures is:

$$C_0 + \frac{X - F_T}{(1 + R_f)^T} = P_0$$

The Black model can be used to price European options on forwards and futures. The price of a European option on a forward or futures contract is equal to an option on the underlying asset if the options and the forward/futures contract expire at the same time.

Swap Markets and Contracts

Cross-Reference to CFA Institute Assigned Topic Review #51

Pricing vs. Valuation of Swaps

The distinction between pricing and valuing swaps is the same as it is for forward contracts:

- The price of a plain-vanilla swap, for example, is the fixed rate (the swap rate) that makes the present value of the fixed-rate payments equal to the present value of the floating-rate payments. Assuming the fixed rate is set to this rate, the value of the swap to both parties at initiation of the swap is zero.
- After initiation, interest rates change and the present value of the payments on both sides of the plain vanilla swap change. The value of the swap to either party after initiation is the present value of the payments that party will receive less the present value of the payments it will make. Because the swap is a derivative instrument, the total value to both sides must be zero, which means this is a zero-sum game, and the value of one side is the negative of the value of the other side.

Swaps as Combinations of Other Instruments

There is a simple bond transaction that is equivalent to a plain vanilla *interest rate swap*. The fixed payer could gain identical exposure by issuing a fixed-coupon bond and investing the proceeds in a floating rate bond with the same maturity and payment dates. On each payment date, a fixed coupon payment is paid, and the floating rate payment is received.

An *equity swap*, from the perspective of the fixed payer, is equivalent to borrowing at a fixed rate and investing in a stock, a portfolio, or an index. The equivalence is not exact, but close enough as an explanation of the capital markets transactions to approximate the exposure of an equity/fixed swap.

The exposure of a *currency swap* is equivalent to that of issuing a bond in one currency, exchanging the proceeds for another currency at the spot exchange rate, and purchasing a bond denominated in the other currency with the same payment and maturity dates.

Pricing and Valuing a Plain Vanilla Interest Rate Swap

We can price a plain vanilla (fixed-for-floating) interest rate swap by using the insight that the swap is equivalent to issuing a fixed-rate bond and buying an otherwise identical floating rate note. The fixed rate (the swap rate) must be set so that the values of the "replicating" floating-rate bond and the "replicating" fixed-rate bond are the same at swap initiation.

The fixed periodic rate on an *N*-period swap at initiation (as a percentage of the principal value) can be calculated as:

$$C_N = \left(\frac{1 - Z_N}{Z_1 + Z_2 + \ldots + Z_N} \right)$$

where:
Z_N = present value of $1 to be received on the *n*th payment date, of *N* dates

At any payment date, the market value of a swap (to the fixed-rate payer) is the difference between the value of the replicating floating-rate bond and the value of the replicating fixed-rate bond. Since the fixed payer is essentially long a floating-rate bond and short a fixed-rate bond, his position will have positive value only when the fixed-rate bond is trading at a discount to par. This follows from the fact that the floating-rate bond will be valued at par at each payment date.

Between payment dates, we can value the swap by noting that the floating rate at the next payment date will trade at par, so its value prior to the payment date is the present value of the par amount plus the known coupon payment. Commit the following relationships to memory:

value of plain vanilla interest rate swap to *fixed-rate-payer side*
= PV of replicating floating-rate bond – PV of replicating fixed-rate bond

value of plain vanilla interest rate swap to *floating-rate-payer side*
= PV of replicating fixed-rate bond – PV of replicating floating-rate bond

Keep in mind that what we are doing is valuing the interest rate swap by valuing an equivalent position in a fixed-rate bond and floating-rate bond. We calculate the value of the fixed-rate bond as the present value of the expected fixed-rate interest payments and principal payments. We calculate the value of the floating-rate bond the same way. The difference between these two values is the value of the swap. The actual swap, however, doesn't require principal payments, and interest payments are netted.

Pricing and Valuing a Currency Swap

Pricing a currency swap (i.e., determining the swap fixed rate in a currency swap) is accomplished using the same procedure as for interest rate swaps, except that now we have to deal with two term structures (one in each currency) and two swap rates.

For example, in a fixed-for-fixed currency swap where one side pays U.S. dollars fixed and the other side pays Euros fixed, the U.S. dollar fixed rate is determined using the term structure of U.S. dollar rates, and the Euro fixed rate is determined from the term structure of Euro rates.

Valuing a currency swap is also similar to valuing an interest rate swap; we value the "replicating bonds" for each side of the swap, and then the value to each party is calculated as the value of the payments it receives less the value of the payments it makes. However, there is the complicating factor of dealing with two different currencies and an exchange rate between the two currencies that changes over time.

Let's use the fixed-for-fixed U.S. dollar-Euro swap as an example to illustrate the procedure, assuming we are valuing the swap in U.S. dollars.

- Given the notional principal of the swap in dollars, convert to Euros using the exchange rate at the initiation of the swap. The notional principal in dollars is the face value of the replicating U.S. dollar denominated bond; the notional principal in Euros is the face value of the replicating Euro denominated bond.
- After the initiation of the swap, value the U.S. dollar-denominated bond in U.S. dollars and the Euro-denominated bond in Euros using the usual procedure.
- Convert the value of the Euro denominated bond into U.S. dollars using the exchange rate in effect on the date the swap is being valued (which will most likely be different than the original rate used to calculate the notional principals).
- Calculate the value of the swap to each party as the difference between the U.S. dollar values of the two bonds. For example, the value of the swap to the party paying U.S. dollars is the value of the Euro-denominated bond (in U.S. dollars) minus the value of the U.S. dollar-denominated bond (in U.S. dollars).

Equity Swaps

The fixed-rate side of an equity swap is priced and valued just like an interest rate swap. The equity side can be valued by multiplying the notional amount of the contract times one plus the percentage equity appreciation since the last payment date. Use the difference in values to value the swap.

Credit Risk

Credit risk arises because of the possibility that the other party to a swap cannot or will not make the payments required by the swap contract. Several key points to remember include:

- Current credit risk is the credit risk associated with the payment currently due.
- Potential credit risk reflects the future credit risk remaining over the life of the swap.
- For an interest rate swap, potential credit risk is greatest in the middle of the swap term when the credit worthiness of the counter party may have deteriorated since swap initiation, and there are significant payments yet to be made over the remaining term of the swap.
- For a currency swap, the maximum potential credit risk occurs after the middle of the swap term because of the remaining principal payment due at maturity.
- Credit risk can be reduced by:
    - Netting.
    - Marking to market.

Swaptions

A *payer swaption* is the right to enter into a specific swap at some date in the future as the fixed rate payer at a rate specified in the swaption. If swap fixed rates increase (as interest rates increase), the right to enter the pay-fixed side of a swap (a payer swaption) becomes more valuable.

The value of a payer swaption at expiration (if it is in-the-money) is the present value of the difference between swap fixed-rate payments based on the higher existing swap rate and payments based on the strike rate.

A *receiver swaption* is the right to enter into a specific swap at some date in the future as the floating-rate payer at a rate specified in the swaption. A receiver swaption becomes more valuable if rates decrease.

The value of a receiver swaption at expiration (if it is in-the-money) is the present value of the difference in swap fixed-rate payments based on the higher strike rate and the lower existing swap rate.

Uses of Swaptions

A swaption can be used to:

- Hedge an anticipated exposure to fixed or floating interest rate payments.

- Speculate on the direction of interest rates.
- Provide a method of exiting an existing swap prior to the normal termination date.

The *swap spread* is the spread between the swap rate and the comparable maturity T-notes. The swap spread will respond to the same factors as other "quality" spreads.

Interest Rate Derivative Instruments

Cross-Reference to CFA Institute Assigned Topic Review #52

Caps, Floors, and Collars

- An *interest rate cap* is an agreement in which one party agrees to pay the other at regular intervals over a certain period of time when the benchmark interest rate (e.g., LIBOR) exceeds the strike rate specified in the contract. This strike rate is called the cap rate. Because an interest rate cap is a multi-period agreement, a cap is actually a portfolio of call options on LIBOR, called caplets. A long cap is also equivalent to a portfolio of long put options on fixed-income security prices.
- An *interest rate floor* is an agreement in which one party agrees to pay the other at regular intervals over a certain time period when the benchmark interest rate (e.g., LIBOR) falls below the strike rate specified in the contract. This strike rate is called the floor rate. Because a floor is a multi-period agreement, a floor is actually a portfolio of put options on LIBOR, called floorlets. A long floor is also equivalent to a portfolio of long call options on fixed-income security prices.
- An *interest rate collar* is a simultaneous position in a floor and a cap on the same benchmark rate over the same period with the same settlement dates. There are two types of collars. The first type of collar is to purchase a cap and sell a floor to hedge a floating rate liability. The second type of collar is to purchase a floor and sell a cap to hedge a floating rate asset.

Credit Derivatives: An Overview

Cross-Reference to CFA Institute Assigned Topic Review #53

CDS

A **credit default swap** (CDS) is essentially an insurance contract. The **reference obligation** is the fixed income security on which the swap is written—usually a bond but potentially also a loan. If default occurs on the reference obligation, the *protection buyer* receives a payment from the *protection seller*. To obtain this coverage, the protection buyer pays the seller a premium that is either paid upfront or over a period of time. The protection seller is assuming (i.e., long) credit risk and the protection buyer is short credit risk. The swap premium is also referred to as the **CDS spread**.

Risks of CDS

The protection seller is exposed to *counterparty risk* because the protection buyer may fail to deliver the required premium payments. This is a concern when market CDS spreads are lower than the contracted spread.

The protection buyer is exposed to the risk that the counterparty defaults; this is termed *replacement risk* because the protection buyer must replace the protection at market prices when the seller fails during the term of the CDS. Replacement risk for a buyer is a concern when market CDS spreads are higher than the contracted spread.

The protection buyer may be exposed to *basis risk* if the reference obligation in the swap differs from the portfolio asset of the buyer.

Finally, the protection buyer is exposed to the risk that the counterparty and the reference entity both default simultaneously; this is termed *double default* risk.

Relation to Other Swaps

A **total return swap** is similar to an equity swap: one party agrees to pay a fixed or floating interest rate and the other party agrees to pay the total return on a bond or bond portfolio. This type of swap transfers both credit risk and market risk.

An **asset swap** is similar to a credit derivative that is constructed by combining a fixed rate bond and a matching pay-fixed interest rate swap. This structure essentially changes the fixed rate bond position into a floating rate bond. Cash flows are illustrated in Figure 8.

Figure 8: Asset Swap

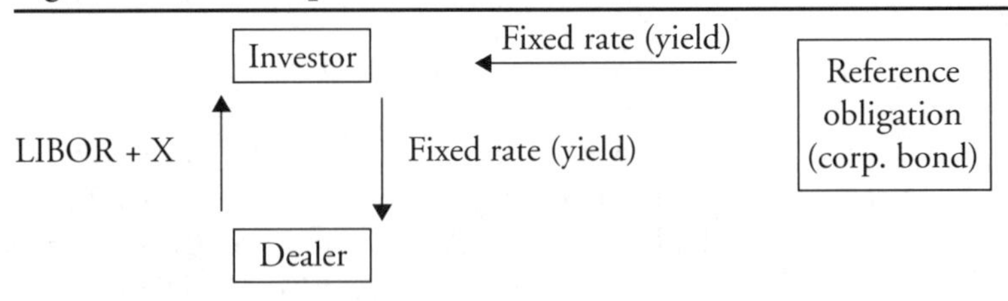

X = asset swap spread = fixed rate on reference obligation – swap fixed rate

The bond yield includes both a premium for credit risk and a premium for interest rate risk (ignoring any liquidity premium). By combining the bond with an interest rate swap, the bondholder has eliminated the interest rate risk. If the bond had no credit risk, the expected LIBOR payments would offer the same overall yield as the promised fixed payments stream; the margin above LIBOR in an asset swap thus compensates the bondholder for bearing the credit risk of the bond. Ignoring counterparty risk on the interest rate swap, the spread above LIBOR (called the asset swap spread; *X* in Figure 8) should be the same as the CDS spread because both capture the default risk premium (i.e., credit spread).

Uses of CDS

CDS can be used to take long or short positions in credit risk, in order to hedge an existing position, speculate on credit spread changes, or to exploit arbitrage opportunities.

CDS Spread

Arbitrage forces CDS spreads to equal asset swap spreads. An alternative method of estimating a CDS spread is to calculate the CDS spread that equates the present value of expected swap premiums to the present value of expected credit loss payments. This method requires assumptions about (estimates of) both the probability of default in each period and the loss as a percentage of the notional value of the swap in the case of default.

CDS spreads are positively related to both the probability of default of the reference entity and to the amount of loss given default.

Dealer Risk Management

Dealers can hedge their long credit risk exposure through offsetting transactions:

- In the inter-dealer market.
- With another client.
- In the cash and interest rate swap market (i.e., replicating an asset swap).

If the reference obligation differs between the hedge and the original swap, basis risk may remain. Additionally, counterparty risk will remain.

Portfolio Management

Study Session 18

Topic Weight on Exam	5–15%
SchweserNotes™ Reference	Book 5, Pages 149–244

Portfolio Concepts

Cross-Reference to CFA Institute Assigned Topic Review #54

Expected Return and Standard Deviation for a Portfolio

The expected return for a 2-asset portfolio is calculated as:

$$E(R_P) = w_1E(R_1) + w_2E(R_2)$$

The variance and standard deviation of a 2-asset portfolio are calculated as:

$$\sigma_p^2 = w_1^2\sigma_1^2 + w_2^2\sigma_2^2 + 2w_1w_2\rho_{1,2}\sigma_1\sigma_2$$

$$\text{and } \sigma_p = \sqrt{\sigma_p^2}$$

The variance and standard deviation of a portfolio of three assets:

$$\sigma_P^2 = w_1^2\sigma_1^2 + w_2^2\sigma_2^2 + w_3^2\sigma_3^2 + 2w_1w_2\text{cov}(1,2) + 2w_1w_3\text{cov}(1,3) + 2w_2w_3\text{cov}(2,3)$$

$$\sigma_P^2 = w_1^2\sigma_1^2 + w_2^2\sigma_2^2 + w_3^2\sigma_3^2 + 2w_1w_2\rho_{1,2}\sigma_1\sigma_2 + 2w_1w_3\rho_{1,3}\sigma_1\sigma_3 + 2w_2w_3\rho_{2,3}\sigma_2\sigma_3$$

$$\sigma_P = \sqrt{\sigma_P^2}$$

The Minimum-Variance Frontier

The *minimum-variance frontier* presented in Figure 1 is the expected return-variance combinations of the set of portfolios that have the minimum variance for every given expected return.

To derive the minimum variance frontier, we must: estimate the risk-return attributes of all assets, run an optimizer that selects portfolio weightings that minimize portfolio variance subject to expected return constraints, and calculate and graph the risk and return for the minimum variance portfolios.

The efficient frontier is the positively sloped portion of the minimum-variance frontier. Portfolios on the efficient frontier have the highest expected return at each given level of risk.

The minimum variance frontier and efficient frontier are unstable because expected returns, variances, and covariances change over time. This is problematic and may lead to large portfolio weighting errors.

Figure 1: Minimum Variance Frontier: Expected Return vs. Variance

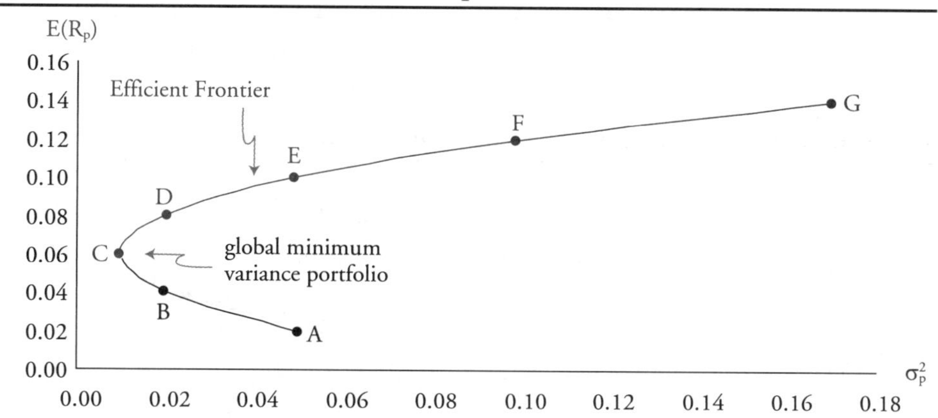

Effect of Correlation and Diversification

Portfolio diversification refers to the strategy of reducing risk by combining different types of assets into a portfolio. Diversification benefits increase as the correlations among assets decrease, and as the number of assets included in the portfolio increase (but portfolio risk falls at a decreasing rate as the size of the portfolio increases).

Figure 2 illustrates how the risk-return profiles of portfolios combining domestic stocks (DS) with domestic bonds (DB) are affected by changes in the correlations. In Figure 3, we include international stocks, which are assumed to have a relatively low correlation with both DS and DB.

Figure 2: Effects of Correlation on Portfolio Risk

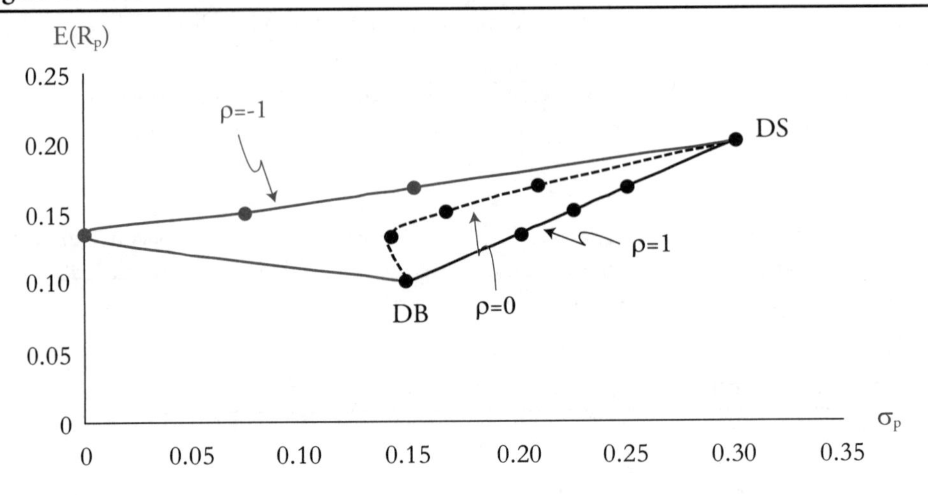

Figure 3: Effect of Number of Assets on Diversification

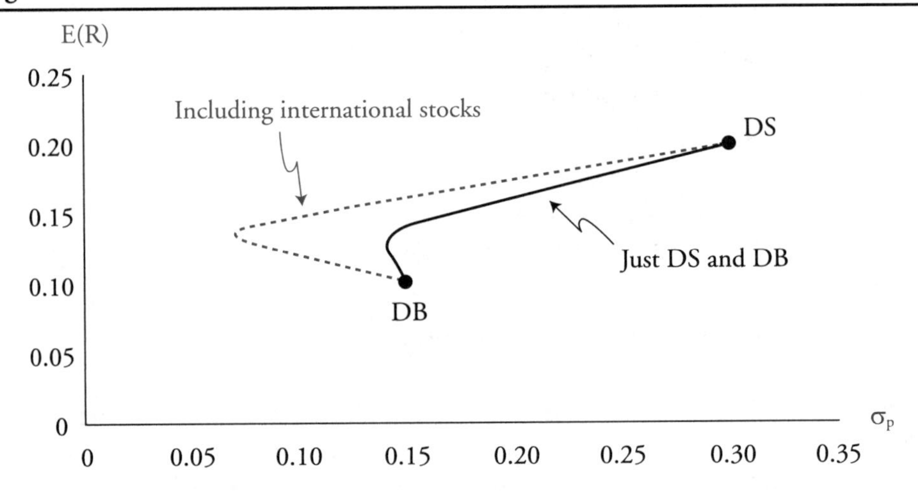

Equally Weighted Portfolio Risk

The most important point to remember is that the variance of an equally-weighted portfolio approaches the average covariance as *n* gets large.

The variance of an equally-weighted portfolio is:

$$\sigma_p^2 = \frac{1}{n}\overline{\sigma_i^2} + \frac{n-1}{n}\overline{\text{Cov}} = \overline{\sigma_i^2}\left(\frac{1-\rho}{n} + \rho\right)$$

We can use the previous formula to illustrate two important concepts:

1. Most of the risk-reduction benefits from diversification can be achieved by adding a relatively small number of stocks to the portfolio.
2. The higher the average correlation, the fewer stocks it takes to achieve a specified amount of risk reduction.

The maximum amount of risk reduction occurs when the number of stocks is very large.

The Capital Allocation Line and the Capital Market Line

In Figure 4, the return on T-bills is shown on the y-axis at 6% (6% return and zero standard deviation). Any combination of the risk-free asset and a risky portfolio with positive weights will fall on a straight line between the two.

Figure 4: Capital Allocation Line

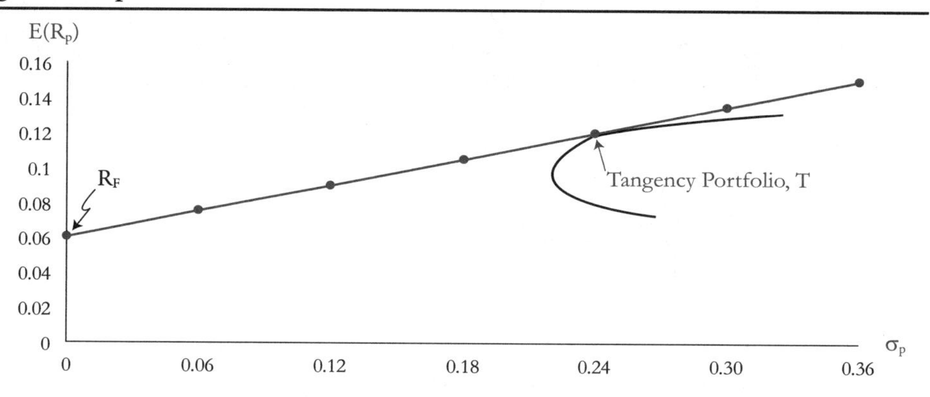

The **capital allocation line** (CAL) is the line from the risk-free rate to the point of tangency on the efficient frontier.

The point of tangency between the CAL and the efficient frontier represents the **best risky portfolio** because when it is combined with a risk-free asset, it is optimal in the sense that it has the highest possible reward-to-risk ratio:

$$\frac{E(R_T) - R_F}{\sigma_T}$$

The reward-to-risk ratio can also be viewed as the expected risk premium $E(R_T) - R_F$ for each unit of risk, σ_T, and is the Sharpe ratio for portfolio T.

The CAL equation:

$$E(R_C) = R_F + \left(\frac{E(R_T) - R_F}{\sigma_T}\right)\sigma_C$$

Here's what you need to remember about the CAL:

- If a risk-free investment is available, investors can combine it with a risky portfolio to increase their return at all levels of risk.
- The CAL is the straight line that intersects the *y*-axis at the risk-free rate and lies tangent to the efficient frontier.
- The intercept of the CAL equals the risk-free rate, and the slope equals the maximum portfolio reward-to-risk ratio, defined as $[E(R_T) - R_F]/\sigma_T$.
- The tangency portfolio is the optimal risky portfolio because it has the highest possible expected reward-to-risk tradeoff.
- The CAL can be used to determine the risk associated with any desired target return, or the expected return associated with any desired target standard deviation that falls on the CAL line.
- The intercept and slope of the CAL depend on the asset expectations of the investor. Therefore, investors with different asset expectations will face different CALs.

If the market portfolio (M) is the tangency portfolio, the CML equation becomes:

$$E(R_C) = R_F + \left(\frac{E(R_M) - R_F}{\sigma_M}\right)\sigma_C$$

The key conclusion of the CML is that all investors will make optimal investment decisions by allocating between the risk-free asset and the market portfolio.

Differences Between the CAL and the CML

Although the CAL and CML are generated using exactly the same mean-variance calculations, there are a few important differences:

- There is only one CML, because it is developed assuming all investors agree on the expected return, standard deviation, and correlations for all assets.
- There is an unlimited number of CALs, because each is developed uniquely for each investor.
- The tangency portfolio for the CML is the *market* portfolio, and there is only one market portfolio. The market portfolio uses market value weights.
- The tangency portfolio for the CAL can differ across investors depending on differences in investor expectations.
- The CML is a special case of the CAL.

CAPM

The **CAPM** calculates the expected return for an asset based on its level of systematic (market-related) risk.

The CAPM equation (also referred to as the SML):

$$E(R_i) = R_F + \beta_i[E(R_M) - R_F]$$

Figure 5: Key Differences Between the SML and the CML

	SML	*CML*
Measure of risk	Uses systematic risk (non-diversifiable risk).	Uses standard deviation (total risk).
Application	Tool used to determine the appropriate expected (benchmark) returns for securities.	Tool used to determine the appropriate asset allocation (percentages allocated to the risk-free asset and to the market portfolio) for the investor.
Definition	Graph of the capital asset pricing model.	Graph of the efficient frontier.
Slope	Market risk premium.	Market portfolio Sharpe ratio.

Beta is a measure of an asset's systematic risk:

$$\text{beta} = \frac{\text{cov}(i, M)}{\sigma_M^2} = \frac{\rho_{i,M}\sigma_i\sigma_M}{\sigma_M^2} = \frac{\sigma_i}{\sigma_M}\rho_{i,M}$$

The **market model** is the regression model often used to estimate betas for common stocks. Specifically, it defines the return to Asset *i*, R_i as:

$$R_i = \alpha_i + \beta_i R_M + \varepsilon_i$$

The market model makes three predictions:

1. $E(R_i) = \alpha_i + \beta_i E(R_M)$
2. $\sigma_i^2 = \beta_i^2\sigma_M^2 + \sigma_{\varepsilon_i}^2$
3. $\text{Cov}_{ij} = \beta_i\beta_j\sigma_M^2$

Adjusted Beta

Historical betas may be very poor predictors of future betas. The beta instability problem is addressed by adjusting the beta to account for its tendency to gravitate to a value of 1 over time.

The general form of the "adjusted beta" equation can be presented as:

$$\text{forecast } \beta_{i,t} = \alpha_0 + \alpha_1 \beta_{i,t-1}$$

where:
the sum of $\alpha_0 + \alpha_1$ is set equal to 1

Blume suggested values of α_0 and α_1 are $\alpha_0 = 1/3$ and $\alpha_1 = 2/3$.

Multifactor Models

1. *Macroeconomic factor models* use unexpected changes (surprises) in macroeconomic variables to explain asset returns.
2. *Fundamental factor models* assume asset returns are explained by the returns from multiple firm-specific factors.
3. *Statistical factor models* determine which "factors" best explain returns on a cross section of securities.

The following model is an example of a 2-factor macroeconomic model in which stock returns are a function of unexpected changes in inflation and GDP.

$$R_i = a_i + b_{i1}F_{INF} + b_{i2}F_{GDP} + \varepsilon_i$$

The Macroeconomic Factor Model vs. the Fundamental Factor Model

The key differences between the macroeconomic factor model and the fundamental factor model can be summarized as follows:

- *Sensitivities.* The standardized sensitivities in the fundamental factor model (b_{i1} and b_{i2}) are calculated directly from the attribute (e.g., P/E) data—they are not estimated. This contrasts with the macroeconomic factor model, in which the sensitivities are regression slope estimates.
- *Interpretation of factors.* The macroeconomic factors (F_{GDP} and F_{QS}) are surprises in the macroeconomic variables (e.g., inflation shock and interest rate shock). In contrast, the fundamental factors ($F_{P/E}$ and F_{SIZE}) are rates of return associated with each factor and are estimated using multiple regression.

- *Number of factors.* Macroeconomic factors are intended to represent systematic risk factors, and are usually small in number (parsimonious model). Fundamental factors often are large in number, providing a more cumbersome, yet more detailed, model of the risk-return relationship for assets.
- *Intercept term.* The intercept in the macroeconomic factor model equals the stock's expected return (based on market consensus expectations of the macro factors) from an equilibrium pricing model. In contrast, the fundamental factor model intercept (with standardized coefficients) has no economic interpretation.

APT and Other Factor Models

The **arbitrage pricing theory** (APT) model is an equilibrium asset-pricing model, like the CAPM, except that it makes less-restrictive assumptions.

A *k*-factor model shows that the expected return on a diversified portfolio is linearly related to the factor sensitivities of that portfolio:

$$E(R_p) = R_F + \lambda_1\beta_{p,1} + \ldots + \lambda_k\beta_{p,k}$$

- The APT is an equilibrium-pricing model, while macroeconomic multifactor models are *ad hoc*.
- The intercept term in a macroeconomic factor model is the asset's expected return, while the APT intercept is the risk-free rate.
- In general multifactor models, the factors represent surprises. In the APT, since it is an equilibrium model, the factors are actual risk premiums analogous to the market risk premium in the SML.

Active Risk and Return

Active return is the difference between portfolio and benchmark returns (RP – RB), and active risk is the standard deviation of active return over time. Active risk is determined by the manager's active factor tilt and active asset selection decisions.

active risk squared = active factor risk + active specific risk

Information Ratio

The information ratio is active return divided by active risk:

$$IR = \frac{\bar{R}_P - \bar{R}_B}{s_{(R_P - R_B)}}$$

Uses of Factor and Tracking Portfolios

- A *factor portfolio* is a portfolio that has been constructed to have sensitivity equal to 1.0 to only one risk factor.
- A *tracking portfolio* is constructed to have the same factor exposures as a benchmark. The manager generates alpha through security selection.

CAPM and APT

The CAPM is a single-factor asset pricing model, in which only risk relative to the broad market is priced. The CAPM suggests that all investors should hold some combination of the market portfolio and the risk-free asset. In contrast, the APT captures multiple dimensions of risk besides the overall market risk, and suggests that investors make decisions relative to multiple sources of risk.

Investors who are independently wealthy and do not depend on their salary as a source of income can earn a substantial risk premium by increasing their portfolio allocation to cyclical stocks, even though they are exposed to less-than-average systematic recession risk.

The Theory of Active Portfolio Management

Cross-Reference to CFA Institute Assigned Topic Review #55

Active portfolio management refers to decisions of the portfolio manager to actively manage and monitor the broad asset allocation and security selection of the portfolio. The theory of active portfolio management can be justified:

- *Economically*. In an efficient market, investors will allocate funds to passively managed (indexed) portfolios. But as less money is actively managed, asset prices may begin to deviate from fair values, which, in turn, will attract transfers of cash flows into actively managed funds.
- *Empirically*. Some portfolio managers have demonstrated abnormally strong performance over extended periods. Consequently, investors seek actively managed funds that they think will be among the star performers.

Treynor-Black Model and Its Use

The Treynor-Black model is a portfolio optimization framework that combines modern portfolio theory and market inefficiency. The model is based on the premise that markets are nearly efficient, and that the number of mispriced assets is limited.

The specific steps in the Treynor-Black model are as follows:

Step 1: Develop capital market expectations (expected return and standard deviation) for the *passively managed* market index portfolio, M.

Step 2: Identify the limited set of mispriced securities, which are securities with large (positive and negative) predicted alphas—defined as the analyst's forecast (expected) return minus the CAPM required return.

Step 3: Determine weightings across the mispriced securities to form the *actively managed* portfolio, A.

The Treynor-Black model penalizes securities that have high unsystematic risk because of the loss of diversification they bring to the investor's total portfolio. The following summarizes the Treynor-Black model allocations within the actively managed Portfolio A:

- Small weight for securities with small alphas and high unsystematic risk.
- Large weight for securities with large alphas and low unsystematic risk.
- Positive weight (long positions) for securities with positive alphas.
- Negative weight (short positions) for securities with negative alphas.

Step 4: Determine weightings to the actively managed Portfolio A and to the passively managed market index M to form *optimal Portfolio P*. Portfolio P is the combination of portfolios A and M that will have the highest possible Sharpe ratio (higher than both Portfolio A or M).

Figure 6 illustrates the optimization process leading to the selection of optimal risky Portfolio P.

Figure 6: The Treynor-Black Optimal Risky Portfolio

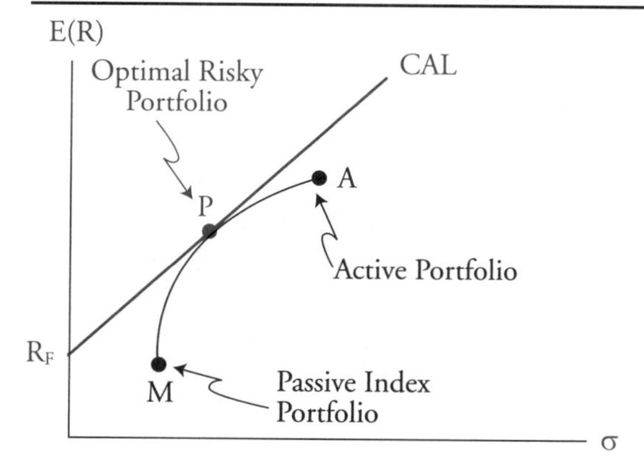

Step 5: Allocate funds to Portfolio P and to the risk-free asset that satisfies the investor's risk aversion. The investor's optimal investment (combination of risk-free asset and risky Portfolio P) is represented by the tangency point of the investor's indifference curve with the capital allocation line (point C in Figure 7).

Figure 7: The Treynor-Black Optimal Risky and Risk-Free Allocation

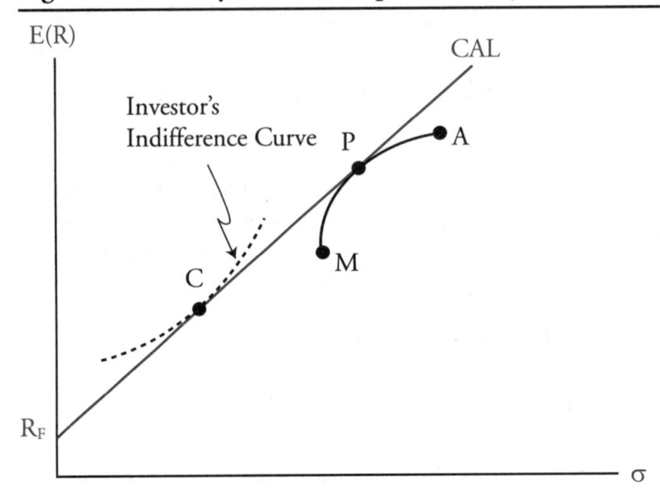

Treynor-Black Calculations

The following is a summary of the key equations used in the Treynor-Black model for an actively managed portfolio comprising two assets:

Stock Alphas

$$\alpha_i = \text{forecast return for stock i} - \{R_F + \beta_i[E(R_M - R_F]\}$$

Weightings Within the Actively Managed Portfolio A

The weight of an individual security in the active portfolio A is positively related to that security's alpha and negatively related to its unsystematic risk. Because the weights of all securities add up to 1, we can also state that the weight of an individual security in the active portfolio A is negatively related to the alpha of the other securities in the active portfolio and positively related to their unsystematic risk.

Portfolio A Alpha

$$\alpha_A = \text{forecast return for Portfolio A} - \{R_F + \beta_A[E(R_M - R_F]\}$$

or, equivalently, the weighted average of the individual security alphas:

$$\alpha_A = w_1\alpha_1 + w_2\alpha_2$$

Incorporating Analyst Forecast Accuracy

The Treynor-Black weightings within the actively managed portfolio can be adjusted for the forecasting ability exhibited by the analyst. To make the proper adjustments, we rely on regression analysis. For the Treynor-Black alpha forecasts, the R^2 equals the percentage of the changes in the realized alpha that are explained by changes in the forecast alpha, or vice versa—the realized alpha (depending on which variable we use for the dependent variable). The main point is that we can adjust the analyst's alpha to control for his forecasting accuracy. The specific steps are as follows:

- Collect the time-series alpha forecasts for the analyst.
- Calculate the correlation between the alpha forecasts and the realized alphas.
- Square the correlation to derive the R^2.
- Adjust (shrink) the forecast alpha by multiplying it by the analyst's R^2.

The Portfolio Management Process and the Investment Policy Statement

Cross-Reference to CFA Institute Assigned Topic Review #56

Steps of the Portfolio Management Process

There are three steps of the portfolio management process: (1) planning, (2) execution, and (3) feedback. The *components of the planning phase* include:

- Analyzing objectives and constraints.
- Developing an investment policy statement.
- Determining the appropriate investment strategy.
- Selecting an appropriate asset allocation.

Investment Objectives

Risk objectives are those factors associated with an investor's willingness and ability to take risk. Combining willingness and ability to accept risk is termed *risk tolerance*. Risk aversion indicates an investor's inability and unwillingness to take risk.

Willingness to tolerate risk is determined by psychological factors (i.e., subjective factors). For example, clients might feel their portfolios are large or that they are better than others at interpreting market or firm information. Other people are just naturally "risk takers." When a client makes statements about risk tolerance, you should interpret the statements as indicators of willingness, not ability, to tolerate risk. Always consider what the client does.

The client's *ability to tolerate risk* is jointly determined by the size of the portfolio (not the client's perception of the size of the portfolio), the client's time horizon, and the client's spending (i.e., liquidity) needs.

Guidelines on ability to tolerate risk:

- As the size of the portfolio increases → ability increases (*positive* relationship).
- As the time horizon increases → ability increases (*positive* relationship).
- As liquidity needs increase → ability decreases (*negative* relationship).
- If willingness > ability → must reconcile the difference by educating client.
- If willingness < ability → must reconcile the difference by educating client.

Return objectives are classed as either desired return (as stated by the client) or required return (as determined by financial obligations). Return objectives should be consistent with the investor's risk objectives. The objectives should differentiate between real and nominal returns, and pre-tax and after-tax returns. The return objective should be considered from a *total return perspective* reflecting both income and capital gains.

Investment Constraints

Liquidity constraints relate to expected or unexpected cash flows needed in the future. The liquidity constraint is closely linked to the risk and return objectives because liquidity needs will influence the ability to take risk and reduce expected return objectives.

Time horizon constraints are associated with the time period(s) during which the portfolio is expected to generate returns. There is also a link between time horizon constraints and risk objectives: long time horizons increase the investor's ability to take risk (although not necessarily the willingness to take risk).

Tax constraints depend on how, when, and if portfolio returns of various types are taxed. Investment choices must be made with careful consideration of how a portfolio's returns will be taxed.

Legal and regulatory constraints mainly affect institutional investors. The Prudent Investor Rule is an example of a legal constraint facing trustees.

The investor's *unique circumstances* are investment constraints that do not fit neatly in any of the other four categories.

Figure 8: Investment Objectives of Individual and Institutional Investors

Investor	*Return Requirement*	*Risk Tolerance*
Individual investor	Depends on life cycle stage and financial position	Depends on life cycle stage and financial position
Defined benefit pension plan	Sufficient to fund pension liability while accounting for inflation	Depends on plan features, age of workforce, and funding status of plan
Defined contribution pension plan	Depends on life cycle stage of beneficiaries	Depends on risk tolerance of beneficiaries
Endowments and foundations	Sufficient to cover spending needs, expenses, and inflation	Generally average or above average
Life insurance companies	Function of policy holder reserve rates	Below average because of significant regulatory constraints
Non-life insurance companies	Function of policy pricing and financial strength	Below average because of significant regulatory constraints
Banks	Function of cost of funds	Depends on business model and financial strength

Investment Policy Statement (IPS)

The IPS is a formally written document providing guidelines for portfolio investment decision making. The IPS does the following:

- Provides guidance for current and possibly subsequent investment adviser decisions.
- Promotes long-term discipline in investment decision making.
- Protects against short-term shifts in strategy when either market conditions or portfolio performance cause panic or overconfidence.

There are several elements to a suitable IPS: a description of the client's situation; the purpose, as well as identification, of responsibilities; formal statements of objectives and constraints; schedule of portfolio performance and IPS review; asset allocation ranges; and guidance for rebalancing and adjustment activities are usually found in an appropriately generated IPS.

Strategic Asset Allocation

The three common approaches to investing are:

1. *Passive investment strategies,* which include indexing and buy-and-hold strategies.
2. *Active investment strategies,* which include managing for a positive alpha and investing according to a specific style or in a specific industry or sector.
3. *Semi-active, risk-controlled active, or enhanced active strategies,* which include index tilting, where the manager over- or under-weights certain sectors of the index based on capital market expectations.

The final strategic asset allocation across asset classes reflects the investment policy statement and capital market expectations.

Essential Exam Strategies

Game Plan

This chapter provides important guidance about *how* to pass the Level II CFA exam. These insights and techniques will help you successfully demonstrate your hard-earned knowledge on exam day.

There are some important differences between preparing for the Level II exam and the Level I exam. First, the question format will be different. The entire Level II exam will be multiple-choice questions in an item set format. Item sets are short cases, usually about one or two pages in length, followed by a series of six questions on the material in the case. Both the morning and the afternoon sessions will include ten item sets each.

On the Level II exam, you are expected to demonstrate a greater depth of understanding than on the Level I exam, so success at Level I is no guarantee of success at Level II.

We begin by showing you some proven approaches to mastering the Level II CFA curriculum. Next, we will communicate a plan for the last week before the exam. We will offer important suggestions to make sure you are prepared on exam day—that you're not so flustered by the time you begin the exam that your performance is negatively affected. We will also spend some time discussing strategies for taking the exam and approaching individual questions.

The Practice Field

As you prepare for the CFA exam, try to focus on the exam itself. Don't add to your stress level by worrying about whether or not you'll pass or what might happen if you don't. If you must, you can worry about all of that *after* the exam. Your performance will suffer if you worry about it before or during the exam. There is ample stress in remembering so much material—you certainly do not need to add more. Many of the tips we provide are proven exam-day stress reducers. Your grasp of the content, combined with our test-taking tips, should have you very well prepared for the exam. You will be ready for the questions, and you will be ready for the exam experience.

All of the faculty at Kaplan Schweser have earned the CFA charter and have extensive experience teaching the topics covered in the CFA curriculum. We know what you are experiencing, and we have witnessed thousands of candidates go through the process of earning the right to use the CFA designation. Now, we want to share with you the time-honored strategies that we have personally seen lead to success on the Level II exam.

There are two fundamentals for success on the Level II exam: focus on the big picture and know the main concepts.

The Big Picture

Focusing on the big picture means you should know something about as many concepts as possible. For example, many candidates are not comfortable with pension accounting, because it seems to them like a lot of adjustments that do not make a big difference in analyzing a stock. Our advice is to learn some of the basics for the exam. For example, learn the differences between IFRS and U.S. GAAP in recognizing pension expense in income statement versus OCI. By remembering some basic information on exam day, you will be able to narrow your answer choices on an item set. You probably won't get every question correct with only a basic grasp of the concept, but you can help yourself out. You can improve your odds on a multiple-choice question from 33% to 50% by eliminating one incorrect answer choice. Also, you will be better able to discriminate between relevant and irrelevant information in a question.

Another component of the big picture focus is studying as many topics as possible. Even if you never use futures contracts, you know you never will, and you don't want to waste time studying them, try to get at least a basic grasp of important concepts. It is a very poor exam strategy to ignore significant pieces of the curriculum. Some candidates believe that as long as they know a few topics very well, they can bluff their way through the rest of the exam. These may be smart people, but their exam strategy isn't smart.

Know the Main Concepts

By knowing the main concepts, we mean identifying the "must know" Level II concepts. With the help of many experienced folks here at Kaplan Schweser, we have done some of that in the previous chapters of this book. These are the concepts that we think you have to know to be successful on the Level II exam. In any given year, some of these concepts might be omitted, but if you can answer every question on these concepts, you can dramatically increase your odds of passing the exam. Generally, the idea is to be correct on most of the questions on important concepts, and then rely on your "big picture" knowledge to get points on the remaining material.

Topic Weighting

In preparing for the exam, you must pay attention to the weights assigned to each topic in the curriculum. The topic weights are as follows:

Topic	Exam Weight
Ethical and Professional Standards	10%
Quantitative Methods	5–10%
Economics	5–10%
Financial Reporting and Analysis	15–25%
Corporate Finance	5–15%
Equity	20–30%
Alternative Investments	5–15%
Fixed Income	5–15%
Derivatives	5–15%
Portfolio Management	5–15%
Total	**100%**

Formulas

There are many areas where you will need a comprehensive grasp of the material. The big picture approach will help you master large parts of the curriculum, but there is material that will be tested in detail. However, in recent years, the emphasis has shifted away from blindly memorizing formulas and then plugging numbers into them and grinding out an answer. Instead, you also need to know in which situations the formula can be applied appropriately and the assumptions that support it. Being able to work with and interpret formulas will be important to your exam day success, but don't focus on simply memorizing them.

Characteristic Lists

A common type of question is one that requires you to identify the characteristics of securities, models, or valuation methods. A typical question format would be "Which of the following most accurately describes …?" Here, the big picture approach can help you eliminate incorrect answers.

Rule Book

At some point in your studies, we recommend that you take time to review the information in the "Candidate Resources" section of CFA Institute Web site (*www.cfainstitute.org*). Believe it or not, you will probably find this to be a nice break from accounting or derivatives! For example, be sure that you are able to comply with the requirements for a government-issued photo ID. Select an approved calculator and learn how to use it. Read the Candidate Bulletins that are issued by CFA Institute in the months before the exam, and be aware of items you can and cannot take to the exam. CFA Institute strictly prohibits taking any of the following into the testing room:

- Food or drinks.
- Backpacks, briefcases, or luggage of any kind.
- Any study materials.
- Scratch paper or calculator manuals.
- Highlighters, rulers, or correction fluid (white-out).
- Cell phones or any personal electronics.

These policies *will* apply to *you*. Every year, many candidates have problems on exam day because they assume their case is a legitimate exception. There is no such thing. We can't tell you how many stories we've heard of candidates sprinting to their cars to put stuff away and getting back just in time to start the exam. If you read the rules and follow them, you will reduce the potential for unexpected stress on exam day.

Final Warm-Ups

You should have a definite strategy for the last week before the exam. If possible, take at least some of the week off from work. You should save at least one practice exam (six hours) for this last week. To simulate the actual exam, avoid looking through or studying this exam until you are ready to sit down and take it for the first time. Take the exam early in the week, and time yourself. Then, use the results to determine where to focus your study efforts over the last few days. You should devote most of your time to areas where you performed poorly, but spend enough time on your stronger topics to keep them fresh in your mind and keep your confidence level up.

Visit the actual exam center sometime during the week before the exam. Determine how long it will take to get there on exam day and where you can park. Even if you are returning to the same site where you took the Level I exam, be sure nothing has changed because of construction or a move to a different floor or room. Locate a nearby lunch destination in the area. The fewer surprises and distractions on exam day, the better. If the exam center has multiple entrances, find out where you will be able to get in on exam day.

Expect problems on exam day. Be prepared for things like cold or hot rooms, noise, or long lines. There are likely to be some of these that you cannot control, but if you are prepared for them, your exam performance is less likely to be affected.

Avoid "binge" studying the evening before the exam. Relax, and make a concerted effort to get a good night's sleep. Tired candidates make silly mistakes on the CFA exam. You will miss easy points if you are not rested. This seems like an obvious and trite point, but it is difficult to overemphasize the importance of going into the exam well-rested.

CFA Institute Question Construction Guidelines

CFA Institute has released very specific guidelines it uses to develop multiple choice questions. We will review the most important issues, but refer to the Candidate Resources section of the CFA Institute Web site (*www.cfainstitute.org*) for more detailed information.

Construction of Multiple Choice Questions

Item set questions on the Level II CFA exam consist of a one- to two-page vignette, a stem (which can be a question, a statement, or a table), and three possible answers labeled A, B, and C. One of the three choices is the correct answer and the other two are incorrect. For example, consider the following question:

A company reports $1,000 in sales, $500 in assets, and $400 in equity. The company's total asset turnover ratio is *closest* to:

A. 0.4.
B. 0.5.
C. 2.0.

The shaded text is the stem and the correct answer is "C" (total asset turnover is sales/assets, or $1,000/$500 = 2.0).

The other two choices are plausible answers that result if you make a common mistake. For example, if you incorrectly calculate total asset turnover as:

- Equity divided by sales, you'll get $400/$1,000 = 0.4, and choose "A."
- Assets divided by sales, you'll get $500/$1,000 = 0.5, and choose "B."

This is an important point: the other two choices are carefully selected to be common errors made by candidates, so don't be lulled into a false sense of security just because your answer happens to show up among the choices.

Word Choice in Stems

According to CFA Institute, stems do not use the following terms:

- EXCEPT.
- TRUE.
- FALSE.

NOT is avoided whenever possible, although it's likely you'll see at least a few questions on the Level II exam that include NOT in the stem.

Many stems, however, do use qualifying words such as:

- *Most* likely.
- *Least* likely.
- *Best* described.
- *Most* appropriate.
- *Most* accurate.
- *Least* appropriate.
- *Least* accurate.

Questions that require a calculation, such that the choices are numerical choices (as in our example), will often use "closest to," so if your calculated answer is close to, but not exactly equal to, any one of the choices, go with the one that's closest to your answer. If you've taken the right approach on the question, your answer will be close to one of the choices, and not nearly as close to any of the others.

Notice that this is consistent with the idea that you should choose the "best" response among the three choices. It is possible, for example, that you could argue that two choices are "appropriate," but only one of them is "most appropriate." In cases where you think more than one choice might be appropriate, always go with the one that best answers the question; don't spend your time creating unlikely scenarios where another choice might just be possible in some unusual circumstance.

CFA Institute does not use any of the following as answer choices:

- All of the above.
- None of the above.
- Cannot determine.
- Cannot calculate.
- Not enough information to determine.

Basic Formats for Multiple-Choice Questions

CFA Institute uses three basic formats to create most (but not all) of the multiple choice questions on the Level II exam.

Example 1 (Stems using sentence completion)

> The price of a European put option on a non-dividend paying stock will *most likely* decrease as a result of a decrease in the:
> A. risk-free rate.
> B. underlying stock price.
> C. volatility of the returns on the underlying stock.

The correct answer is "C" because the put price is positively related to volatility (put vega is positive), so if volatility decreases, the price of the put will also decrease.

Choice "A" is incorrect because the put price is negatively related to the risk-free rate (put rho is negative), so if the risk-free rate decreases, the price of the put will increase.

Choice "B" is incorrect because the put price is negatively related to the underlying stock price (put delta is negative), so if the stock price decreases, the price of the put will increase.

Example 2 (Stems phrased as questions)

> A decrease in which of the following is *most likely* to result in a decrease in the price of a European put option on a non-dividend paying stock?
> A. Risk-free rate.
> B. Underlying stock price.
> C. Volatility of the returns on the underlying stock.

Once again, the answer is "C."

Example 3 ("Yes, No because..." or "No, Yes because...")

Assume that the original data for the labor force participation rate showed a definite upward trend. Kevin Spears took the natural log and first differenced the series and then plotted the differenced data. The plot of the differenced series seems to have constant volatility and appears to fluctuate around a constant mean. Spears' initial conclusion is that the series is covariance stationary. Is this a correct initial conclusion?

A. Yes.
B. No, because a covariance stationary times series does not fluctuate around the mean.
C. No, because a covariance stationary time series does not have constant volatility.

The correct answer is choice "A." A covariance stationary time series is mean reverting and has a constant volatility. Choice "B" is incorrect because a covariance stationary time series does fluctuate around the mean. Choice "C" is incorrect because a covariance stationary time series has constant volatility.

Game Day

How is an Item Set (Selected Response) Different From Level I Multiple Choice?

An item set is a short story, called a vignette, followed by a series of six questions. The Level II exam will consist of ten item sets in the morning, and ten item sets in the afternoon. According to CFA Institute, the vignette is usually about one and one-half pages in length, although some are more than two pages, and a few are less than one page. You will have 18 minutes for each item set (three minutes for each of the six questions), but remember that you must allow time to read and digest the information given. It is generally a good idea to skim through the vignette once, just enough to get the basic idea (without trying to memorize each detail), and then read the questions. As you answer each question, refer back to the vignette to verify your facts and be sure that they support the answer selected.

According to CFA Institute, from 30–40% of the Level II questions will be quantitative, meaning that calculations will be required to determine the answer. The remaining questions will be qualitative, requiring knowledge of how to apply and interpret the concepts in the curriculum. Note that this can include the interpretation of numerical data that is provided for you. Don't expect the qualitative questions to be easier than the quantitative ones.

Answering a Multiple Choice Question in a Level II Item Set

Here are some tips to keep in mind as you work through item set questions:

- Do *not* judge the facts presented in the case. If part of the scenario seems unrealistic, do not twist the facts to fit your "real world" understanding of the topic. Accept the facts as given and answer the questions using the CFA curriculum.
- Read each question carefully! Watch for double negatives, like "All of the following are disadvantages except:" It is very important not to miss words by reading too quickly; for example, don't read "most likely" instead of "least likely."

Professor's Note: One suggestion to keep "least likely" and "most likely" straight on the exam is to cross out "least likely" and put FALSE, and cross out "most likely" and put "TRUE." Always remember, though, that you are looking for the best answer.

- Read *all* answer choices. Don't just stop when you get to one that sounds right; there may be a better choice.
- Identify and underline each piece of relevant information provided in the case and note which points are related to a specific question. Often, a wrong answer looks good because it is consistent with information in the case that was actually irrelevant.
- After you read each question, determine what you think the question is asking and restate it in your own words. This will help you filter out information that may support an incorrect choice and help you focus quickly on appropriate answer choices.
- After you read each question, formulate your own answer before reading the answer choices. Anticipate what you expect the answer to be. This will make the correct answer sound better to you when you see it.
- On calculation problems, after you select an answer choice, pause for a moment and think about whether the answer makes sense. Is the sign (positive or negative) of your answer correct, or does the direction of change make sense?
- Do not look for patterns in a series of answers. Just because the last three questions all had "C" for an answer, do not expect that the next question must be "A." There is no reason to expect that CFA Institute has any preference as to how many questions have one letter answer or another.
- Be *very* sure that you mark your answer in the right place on the answer sheet. If you skip questions or do the topics out of order, be careful to check yourself. Mis-marking can be devastating if you do not catch it soon enough!
- Rely on your first impressions. Most people find that their first impressions are usually correct. It's okay to change an answer, but only do so if you have a good reason. When you come back to a question, you will most likely be tired and

not thinking as clearly. You may even be biased by another question that made you think differently. Be sure you can justify any change!

- Finally, and *most* importantly, *do not lose your confidence*. Nobody gets a perfect score on the CFA exam; it just does not happen. Remember, the passing score is probably about 70%. That means you can miss 30% (108 points) and still pass. Even if you begin to struggle on a few questions (or even five or six in a row), do not lose your confidence. The worst thing you can do is start second-guessing yourself—you will take longer on every question and you may start changing correct answers.

What to Do With a Difficult Question in an Item Set

You will run into questions that give you trouble. You might not understand the question, you may think none of the answers make sense, or you may not know that concept. Here are some tips to follow if you find yourself facing a difficult question:

- If the question does not make sense, or if none of the answers look correct, reread the question to see if you missed something. If you are still unsure, mark an answer choice and move on.
- Look at the other questions in the item set to see if they provide help on the question with which you are struggling. There might be a logical progression in the questions that becomes apparent.
- *Never leave an answer blank*. A blank answer has a maximum point value of zero. A randomly marked answer has an expected value of $0.33 \times 3 = 1.0$ point. You are not penalized for wrong answers.

Time Management: General Comments

Candidates who fail the CFA exam frequently cite time management as their biggest downfall. Here are some tips to help you manage your time wisely:

- Take at least one practice exam and time yourself. This will give you some indication of whether you will have problems on exam day.
- One way to alleviate time pressure is to bank a few minutes by doing an easy topic first. Select a topic with which you feel comfortable, and go there first.
- Do not panic! If you need a short break, put down your pencil and take a few deep breaths. The 30 seconds or so that this will take may help you think clearly enough to answer several additional questions correctly.
- Have a lunch destination planned beforehand. If you talk with other candidates during lunch, do not let their comments influence you. They may say the exam is easier or more difficult than they expected, but they may or may not be correct about how well they are doing.

Index

D

E

F

G

H

I

J

K

L

M

N

O

P

Q

R

S

T

U

V

Y

Z

Notes

Notes

Notes